healthy
everyday
Mediterranean

healthy everyday
Mediterranean

70 delicious recipes designed with nutrition in mind

Introduction 6

Breakfast
16

Nutritious Lunches
34

Midweek Dinners
60

Batch Cooking & Meal Prep
90

Air Fryer & Slow Cooker
114

Savoury Snacks
132

Desserts
150

Conversion Charts 170

Index 171

Introduction

The Mediterranean diet is more than a way of eating, it's a time-tested, nourishing approach to food and health that's inspired by the traditional eating patterns of countries such as Greece, Italy, Spain, southern France, Malta, and Cyprus. Celebrated globally as one of the healthiest and most sustainable dietary patterns, it offers a balanced, enjoyable way to eat, not through restriction, but by embracing real, flavourful food.

Eating Well, for Life

Unlike short-term diets, the Mediterranean way of eating is grounded in long-term health. It's naturally rich in fibre, antioxidants, healthy fats, and protective plant compounds, and consistently ranks top in global dietary recommendations for reducing chronic disease risk and promoting healthy ageing.

A wealth of scientific evidence supports its benefits. People who follow a Mediterranean-style diet have been shown to have a significantly lower risk of developing heart disease and stroke – with some studies suggesting a reduction in cardiovascular events by up to 30 per cent. It's also associated with improved blood-sugar control, reduced risk of certain cancers, and support for a healthy weight.

The diet's high intake of anti-inflammatory foods, such as extra virgin olive oil, oily fish, and a colourful variety of plant foods, is thought to play a key role in these protective effects.

The Mediterranean diet also supports brain health, with observational studies linking it to slower cognitive decline and a lower risk of dementia and Alzheimer's disease. In fact, many of the world's longest-living populations, including those in the so-called "blue zones" – such as Ikaria in Greece and Sardinia in Italy – follow dietary patterns closely aligned with the Mediterranean way of eating, reinforcing its link with longevity and vitality in later life.

The Mediterranean Diet

So, what does this actually look like on your plate? The Mediterranean diet is built around simple, wholesome, and often seasonal ingredients:

* **Vegetables and fruits** in a range of colours.

* **Wholegrains** such as bulgur and wholegrain wheat.

* **Pulses** like chickpeas, lentils, and beans.

* **Healthy protein** from meat, fish, eggs, and dairy.

* **Healthy fats** from extra virgin olive oil, nuts and seeds, and oily fish.

* **Herbs and spices** to enhance flavour without relying on ultra-processed ingredients, as well as contributing to plant-based diversity.

* **Seasonal produce** so that we can enjoy foods at their best.

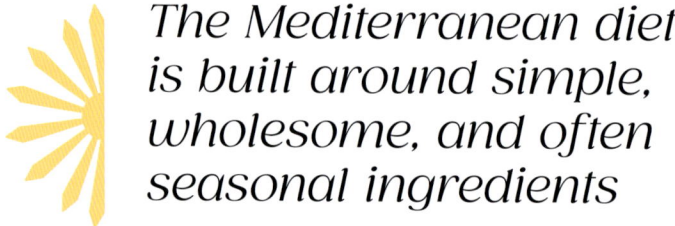

The Mediterranean diet is built around simple, wholesome, and often seasonal ingredients

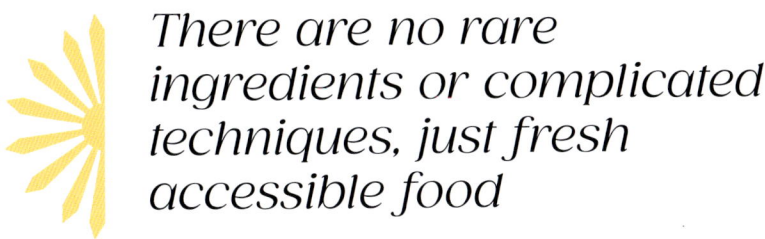

There are no rare ingredients or complicated techniques, just fresh accessible food

Bringing the Med to your Kitchen

This collection is designed to make the Mediterranean diet practical for everyday life. There are no rare ingredients or complicated techniques, just fresh, accessible food you can find in your local supermarket. Each recipe uses affordable staples, such as seasonal vegetables, canned pulses, grains, fish, poultry, eggs, olive oil, nuts, seeds, and dairy – ingredients that are versatile, nutrient-rich, and central to the Mediterranean way of eating.

You'll find dishes like **Spring Green Shakshuka** (see p27), **Watermelon & Halloumi Salad** (see p38), and **Harissa Salmon** (see p74), which showcase the vibrant flavours and variety of plant foods the Mediterranean diet is famous for. Satisfying mains, such as **Chickpea & Halloumi Salad** (see p119) or **Spinach Fritters with Courgette Yogurt** (see p97) highlight the use of wholegrains alongside vegetables, herbs, and heart-healthy olive oil, while **Frittata** (see p32) or **Spanakopita Egg Muffins** (see p23) are examples of high-protein, vegetable-packed options perfect for any time of day.

Focus on Nutrition

To support your confidence in the kitchen, we've included nutritional information for each recipe, highlighting calories, protein, fibre, and both saturated and unsaturated fats. These values aren't about calorie counting or restriction, but about helping you understand how a good balance of foods can be used to support your energy, muscle health, digestion, and long-term wellbeing.

You'll notice an emphasis on heart-healthy unsaturated fats, particularly from extra virgin olive oil, nuts, and oily fish – a hallmark of the Mediterranean diet and a key reason for its cardioprotective effects. Where saturated fat is present, it's often from ingredients like cheese or yogurt. Importantly, dairy provides a unique matrix of nutrients, including calcium, potassium, and high-quality protein – and research suggests that dairy, consumed as part of a balanced dietary pattern, may be cardioprotective.

Fibre is also highlighted as a key feature of the Mediterranean diet. These recipes draw on a wide variety of fibre sources, from vegetables and fruits to wholegrains, pulses, nuts, and seeds, helping to support digestion, blood-sugar control, and a healthy gut microbiome.

The recipe layout makes this information quick to find, so you can choose dishes that suit your needs, whether you're looking for a higher-protein lunch, a fibre-rich dinner, or a heart-healthy balance of fats, and enjoy the Mediterranean diet in a way that's flexible, flavourful, and built to last.

The Mediterranean diet is rooted in tradition, backed by science, and designed to nourish you in body and mind through every stage of life.

Meal Planner

Planning your meals ahead can help you bring Mediterranean balance to your days – and your week. The sample Monday plan comprises colourful fruit and vegetables full of antioxidants, hearty wholegrains from bulgur wheat and quinoa, and salmon rich in omega-3s for a nutritious start to the week.

	MONDAY	TUESDAY	WEDNESDAY
BREAKFAST	French Toast (see p20)		
LUNCH	Cauliflower Salad Bowl (see p47)		
DINNER	Foccacia (see p98), Harrissa Salmon, (see p74)		
SNACKS & SWEETS	Kale Crisps (see p140), Watermelon Granita (see p162)		

THURSDAY	FRIDAY	SATURDAY	SUNDAY

Tips and Tricks

Equipment

It can be useful to have a few pieces of equipment to hand. Here are some handy tools to have in your kitchen:

* **Blender** to make fresh pesto, dressings, dips, and sauces in a matter of seconds.

* **Baking dish** for assembling a variety of lasagnes, traybakes, and parmigianas.

* **Slow cooker** allows you to prepare a week of meals that can be stored in the fridge or frozen, and heated up when short of time.

* **Air fryer** to prepare dishes quickly and easily, without preheating ovens and creating unnecessary washing up.

The larder

And don't forget the unsung hero of the kitchen: the larder. The varied cuisines of the Mediterranean call for a selection of essential store-cupboard staples:

* **Spices** such as cumin, ground coriander, ground cinnamon, and ground turmeric.

* **Jars** of olives, harissa, tahini, peppers, and capers.

* **Pouches** of microwaveable bulgur wheat, couscous, quinoa, and rice.

* **Oils** such as extra virgin olive oil and an olive or vegetable oil spray.

Breakfast

A Mediterranean breakfast is a great way to begin your day with a balanced and nutritious meal. With ingredients that are rich in fibre and full of healthy fats, they offer a stable, satiated start to the day, which will keep you full until lunch.

Figs with Ricotta on Toast

Kcals	442
Protein	24g
Fibre	2g
Saturated Fat	12g
Unsaturated Fat	14g

Serves 4

Prep + cook time:
5 minutes

- 250g (generous 1 cup) ricotta
- 4 thick slices of sourdough
- 4 figs, sliced
- 3 tbsp honey
- 3 sprigs of thyme, leaves picked
- 50g (generous ⅓ cup) walnuts, roughly chopped
- salt

1 Put the ricotta into a blender and blitz until smooth. Set aside.

2 Toast the sourdough bread slices, then spread the ricotta over the toast.

3 Top with the fig slices, drizzle over the honey, sprinkle over the thyme, scatter over the walnuts, add a little salt, and serve.

Swap it Feel free to swap the figs for whatever fruit is in season. Peaches or plums would work well here.

The combination of soft fruit and walnuts provides fibre and antioxidants, while the ricotta adds protein and calcium. Plenty of plant-based omega-3s – to support brain, heart, and anti-inflammatory health – also come from the walnuts.

French Toast

Kcals 345
Protein 13g
Fibre 2.2g
Saturated Fat 3g
Unsaturated Fat 10g

Serves 4

Prep + cook time:
10 minutes

- 4 eggs
- 100ml (6½ tbsp) whole milk
- 1 tsp ground cinnamon
- 1 tsp vanilla extract
- 4 thick slices of bread, slightly stale if possible
- 30g (2 tbsp) unsalted butter, or 2 tbsp extra virgin olive oil
- 50g (1¾oz) raspberries
- 50g (1¾oz) blueberries
- 3½ tbsp maple syrup or honey

1 Crack the eggs into a large, shallow baking dish. Add the milk, cinnamon, and vanilla extract. Whisk together until smooth, then set aside.

2 Place the bread slices into the egg mixture and soak for 2 minutes on each side.

3 Meanwhile, add the butter to a large frying pan set over a medium heat.

4 Remove the bread slices from the dish and add them to the pan. Cook for about 2 minutes on each side until golden in colour. You may need to do this in batches.

5 Place the toast on serving plates, top with the berries, and drizzle over the maple syrup or honey.

Swap it Other fruits, such as figs, bananas, or orange segments, would also work well here.

> The colourful berries added to this protein-rich classic provide a fantastic antioxidant boost.

BREAKFAST

Spanakopita Egg Muffins

Kcals	86
Protein	5.7g
Fibre	0.5g
Saturated Fat	3g
Unsaturated Fat	3g

Makes 12

Prep + cook time:
35 minutes

1 tbsp extra virgin olive oil
1 onion, finely chopped
1 clove of garlic, finely chopped
200g (7oz) spinach, roughly chopped
5 eggs
grated zest of 1 lemon
1 tsp dried oregano
handful of parsley, finely chopped
150g (5¼oz) feta
salt and freshly ground black pepper

1 Preheat the oven to 190°C (170°C fan/375°F/Gas 5).

2 Add the olive oil to a frying pan set over a low–medium heat. Add the onion and cook for 5 minutes until softened. Add the garlic and spinach, then cook for a further 2 minutes until the spinach has just wilted. Take the pan off the heat and set aside.

3 Meanwhile, add the eggs to a bowl and whisk well. Add the spinach mixture, lemon zest, oregano, and parsley, then crumble in the feta. Season with salt and freshly ground black pepper, then mix well and set aside.

4 Line a 12-hole muffin tin with squares of baking parchment, then divide the egg mixture among the muffin holes.

5 Put into the oven and bake for 20–25 minutes until cooked through and a skewer comes out clean when inserted.

Keep it These muffins are great to bake ahead of a busy week – they will keep in the fridge for 4 days.

Eggs and feta provide protein, with leafy spinach adding a boost of iron and fibre. A simple on-the-go way to bring Mediterranean balance to your breakfast.

BREAKFAST

Pan Con Tomate

Kcals 138
Protein 2.8g
Fibre 1.8g
Saturated Fat 1g
Unsaturated Fat 6g

Serves 4

Prep + cook time:
5 minutes

- 2 large tomatoes, halved
- 2 tbsp extra virgin olive oil, plus extra for brushing
- 1 ciabatta loaf, cut into thick slices
- 1 clove of garlic
- handful of chives, chopped
- salt and freshly ground black pepper

1 Grate the tomato flesh into a bowl and discard the skins. Add the olive oil and season with salt and freshly ground black pepper, then mix well and set aside.

2 Preheat the grill.

3 Brush the ciabatta slices with olive oil and arrange on a baking tray. Place under the grill and cook for about 3 minutes until toasted.

4 Rub the ciabatta slices with the clove of garlic, then spoon over the grated tomatoes.

5 Season with a little more salt and freshly ground black pepper, sprinkle over the chives, and serve.

Tip This classic Spanish breakfast is easily adaptable and would also work as part of a summer table for when guests are over. Feel free to add some anchovies or olives for a salty kick.

Grating tomatoes helps release lycopene, a powerful antioxidant that supports heart and skin health. Pairing tomatoes with olive oil improves lycopene absorption in this Spanish-inspired start to the day.

Spring Green Shakshuka

Kcals	393
Protein	28g
Fibre	4g
Saturated Fat	11g
Unsaturated Fat	18g

Serves 2

**Prep + cook time:
15 minutes**

- 1 tbsp extra virgin olive oil, plus extra to drizzle
- 1 onion, finely chopped
- 2 cloves of garlic, finely chopped
- 1 tsp ground cumin
- ½ tsp ground cinnamon
- pinch of chilli flakes
- 1 head of spring greens, tough stalks removed, leaves separated and roughly chopped
- 100g (3½oz) spinach
- 4 eggs
- 100g (3½oz) feta
- grated zest of 1 lemon
- handful of parsley, roughly chopped
- salt and freshly ground black pepper

1 Add the olive oil to a deep frying pan set over a low-medium heat. Add the onion, then cook for 5 minutes until softened.

2 Add the garlic, cumin, cinnamon, and chilli flakes, then cook for a further minute until fragrant.

3 Add the spring greens and spinach and cook for a few minutes until just wilted.

4 Make 4 spaces in the mix with a large spoon, then crack the eggs into the spaces. Cover with a lid and cook for about 4 minutes until the eggs are set.

5 Season with salt and freshly ground black pepper, crumble over the feta, then sprinkle over the lemon zest and parsley. Drizzle over a little olive oil and serve.

Swap it Feel free to adapt this recipe to whatever greens you have in the fridge. You could make this even more simple by using only spinach.

This nourishing dish is packed with leafy greens for magnesium, calcium, iron, and fibre, plus protein from eggs and a calcium boost from feta.

Farinata

Kcals	269
Protein	9g
Fibre	4g
Saturated Fat	3g
Unsaturated Fat	13g

Serves 4

Prep + cook time:
30 minutes, plus resting time

- 150g (1 cup plus 3 tbsp) chickpea flour
- 380ml (scant 1⅔ cups) lukewarm water
- 60ml (¼ cup) extra virgin olive oil
- 2 tbsp finely chopped rosemary, plus extra to serve
- 100g (3½oz) cherry tomatoes, roughly chopped
- handful of parsley, roughly chopped
- handful of basil, roughly chopped
- juice of ½ lemon
- salt and freshly ground black pepper

To serve:
lemon wedges

1 Add the chickpea flour and water to a bowl, and whisk well until smooth. Cover with cling film or a tea towel and set aside for at least 2 hours, or overnight.

2 Preheat the oven to 220°C (200°C fan/425°F/Gas 7).

3 Add 20ml (4 tsp) olive oil into the bowl. Add the rosemary, then season with salt and freshly ground black pepper. Whisk well.

4 Pour 20ml (4 tsp) olive oil into a cast-iron frying pan; place in the oven for 5 minutes to heat up.

5 Remove the pan from the oven, then pour the batter into the pan. Put back into the oven and cook for 20 minutes until lightly golden and cooked through.

6 Meanwhile, to a small bowl, add the tomatoes, parsley, and basil. Drizzle over the remaining 20ml (4 tsp) of olive oil and add the lemon juice. Season with salt and freshly ground black pepper, then mix well and set aside.

7 Remove the farinata from the pan, slice it, and sprinkle on some extra rosemary, salt, and pepper. Serve with the tomato salad and lemon wedges.

Tip This delicious dish makes for the perfect breakfast or brunch. You could also make the whole recipe ahead of time, and simply reheat in the oven when ready to serve.

Made from chickpea flour, this gluten-free flatbread offers plant protein and fibre. Added herbs and tomatoes make it a nutrient-dense, savoury brunch.

Turkish Eggs

Kcals 389
Protein 26g
Fibre 0.6g
Saturated Fat 12g
Unsaturated Fat 18g

Serves 2

Prep + cook time:
20 minutes

- 200g (scant 1 cup) Greek yogurt
- 1 clove of garlic, crushed
- grated zest and juice of ½ lemon
- 30g (2 tbsp) unsalted butter
- 1 tbsp extra virgin olive oil
- 1 tsp Aleppo pepper or paprika
- 1 tbsp white wine vinegar
- 4 eggs
- handful of dill
- salt and freshly ground black pepper

Crispy shallots and garlic (optional):
- 3 tbsp vegetable oil
- 2 banana/echalion shallots, thinly sliced
- 2 cloves of garlic, thinly sliced

1 If making the crispy shallots and garlic, add the vegetable oil to a frying pan set over a medium heat. Add the shallots and fry for 7–10 minutes until golden, then remove with a slotted spoon and drain on kitchen paper. Repeat with the garlic, frying for 2 minutes, then set aside.

2 Bring a large pan of water to a simmer.

3 Meanwhile, to a small bowl, add the yogurt, garlic, lemon zest, and lemon juice. Season with salt and pepper, then mix well and set aside.

4 Add the butter to a small pan set over a low-medium heat. Let the butter melt, foam, then start to brown. Remove from the heat, add the olive oil and Aleppo pepper. Mix well and set aside.

5 Add the vinegar into the simmering water, then create a whirlpool in the water with a spoon. Gently crack in the eggs (you may need to do these in batches). Cook for 3 minutes, remove with a slotted spoon, and set aside on a plate.

6 Spread the yogurt onto 2 plates, then top with the eggs, butter, dill, and crispy shallots and garlic (if using). Season with salt and pepper, and serve.

Tip Get ahead by prepping the yogurt and crispy shallots and garlic the day before.

Greek yogurt provides bone-strengthening calcium, while garlic and shallots offer natural prebiotics for your gut bacteria. Eggs add protein and other key nutrients, such as iron and choline.

BREAKFAST

Frittata

Kcals 358
Protein 28g
Fibre 1g
Saturated Fat 9g
Unsaturated Fat 18g

Serves 2

Prep + cook time:
10 minutes

- 1 tbsp extra virgin olive oil
- 2 spring onions, chopped
- ½ courgette, thinly sliced
- 5 eggs
- handful of basil, roughly chopped
- handful of parsley, roughly chopped
- grated zest of 1 lemon
- 3 tbsp finely grated Parmesan, plus extra to serve
- salt and freshly ground black pepper

1 Add the olive oil to a non-stick frying pan over a low–medium heat. Once hot, add in the spring onions and courgette. Cook for a few minutes until softened.

2 Meanwhile, add the eggs, basil, parsley, most of the lemon zest (reserving a little to serve), and Parmesan to a bowl. Season with salt and freshly ground black pepper, then whisk well.

3 Add the mixture to the frying pan. Swirl the pan round so that the mixture evenly coats the base of the pan. Cook for about 4 minutes until the top is set, then flip out onto a plate, and slide back into the pan, so that the bottom is now on the top. Cook for another few minutes until cooked through.

4 Remove from the frying pan and serve with extra grated Parmesan, lemon zest, and black pepper on top.

Swap it Swap the herbs for whatever you have in the fridge; mint and sage would also work well here.

The eggs provide a brilliant source of protein and iron, with added fibre and flavour from the herbs and veg. This is a satisfying Mediterranean-style way to start your day.

Nutritious Lunches

These Mediterranean recipes will leave you feeling satisfied and help stave off any brain fog throughout the afternoon. From fresh salads, such as Tuna Niçoise, to more hearty pulse-based dishes, such as Gigantes Plaki, there is something here for every appetite.

Gigantes Plaki

Kcals 338
Protein 16g
Fibre 17g
Saturated Fat 2g
Unsaturated Fat 7g

Serves 4

**Prep + cook time:
40 minutes**

- 2 tbsp extra virgin olive oil, plus extra to serve
- 1 onion, finely chopped
- 3 cloves of garlic, crushed
- 2 celery sticks, finely chopped
- 1 tsp ground cinnamon
- 1 tbsp dried oregano
- 2 x 400g (14oz) cans chopped tomatoes
- 2 x 400g (14oz) cans butterbeans, drained and rinsed
- 2 bay leaves
- 1 tbsp red wine vinegar
- 1 tsp caster sugar
- handful of parsley, roughly chopped
- salt and freshly ground black pepper

To serve:
- a few slices of sourdough bread

1 Preheat the oven to 190°C (170°C fan/375°F/Gas 5).

2 Add the olive oil to an ovenproof casserole dish set over a low–medium heat.

3 Add the onion, garlic, and celery to the dish and cook for about 10 minutes until softened.

4 Add the cinnamon, oregano, chopped tomatoes, butterbeans, bay leaves, red wine vinegar, and caster sugar. Cook in the oven, uncovered, for 20 minutes, until thick and bubbling. If it starts to look dry, add in some boiling water.

5 Season generously with salt and freshly ground black pepper, then stir through most of the parsley. Serve topped with the remaining parsley, a drizzle of olive oil, and some bread on the side.

Swap it Feel free to swap the beans for chickpeas or cannellini beans.

Keep it This will keep in the fridge for 5 days, or frozen for 3 months.

> Beans, rich in soluble fibre, are brilliant for gut health and plant protein. When cooked slowly with olive oil and tomatoes, they become even more nourishing and delicious.

NUTRITIOUS LUNCHES

Watermelon & Halloumi Salad

Kcals 493
Protein 15g
Fibre 4.3g
Saturated Fat 9g
Unsaturated Fat 19g

Serves 6

Prep + cook time: 15 minutes

- 2 tbsp sherry vinegar
- 60ml (¼ cup) extra virgin olive oil
- 1 banana/echalion shallot, thinly sliced
- 225g (8oz) block of halloumi, cut into 2cm (¾in) slices
- 1 tbsp honey
- 2 tbsp capers
- 250g (9oz) pouch of microwaveable quinoa
- ½ watermelon, cut into 4cm (1½in) pieces
- ½ cucumber, roughly chopped
- 70g (½ cup) walnuts, roughly chopped
- handful of dill, leaves picked
- handful of basil, roughly chopped
- salt and freshly ground black pepper

1 To a small bowl, add the sherry vinegar, 40ml (2 tbsp plus 2 tsp) olive oil, and shallots. Stir well, then set aside to lightly pickle.

2 Add the remaining 20ml (4 tsp) olive oil to a frying pan set over a medium heat. Add the halloumi slices and fry for about 3 minutes on each side, until golden in colour. Drizzle in the honey, then remove the slices from the pan and set aside.

3 Keep the pan on the heat, then add the capers and cook for 1 minute until crispy. Set aside.

4 Heat the quinoa according to the packet instructions, and allow to cool slightly.

5 To a large bowl, add the watermelon, cucumber, walnuts, quinoa, dill, basil, halloumi, and capers. Season with salt and freshly ground black pepper, then drizzle over the shallot dressing. Toss the salad together and serve.

Swap it This salad is adaptable. Feel free to swap out the halloumi for feta. Swap the herbs for whatever you may have in the fridge. Parsley and fresh oregano would also work well here.

The freshness of watermelon pairs beautifully with the savoury richness of halloumi. Walnuts and herbs add extra texture, plant diversity, and Mediterranean-style heart-health benefits.

Spanish Tortilla

Kcals 335
Protein 11g
Fibre 2.8g
Saturated Fat 4g
Unsaturated Fat 18g

Serves 6

Prep + cook time: 40 minutes

- 80ml (⅓ cup) extra virgin olive oil
- 2 onions, thinly sliced
- 600g (1lb 5oz) waxy potatoes, peeled and thinly sliced
- 6 eggs
- salt and freshly ground black pepper

Green salad:
- 2 tbsp extra virgin olive oil
- juice of 1 lemon
- 100g (3½oz) baby spinach
- 50g (1¾oz) rocket
- handful of dill, leaves picked
- handful of chives, finely chopped
- salt and freshly ground black pepper

1 Add 70ml (5 tbsp) of the olive oil to a 20cm (8in) non-stick frying pan set over a medium heat. Add the onions and cook for about 10 minutes until the onions start to turn golden in colour. Add the potatoes and cook for a further 10–15 minutes until the potatoes have softened.

2 Meanwhile, crack the eggs into a bowl, whisk well, and set aside.

3 Add the potato and onion mixture to the bowl of eggs, then season well with salt and freshly ground black pepper. Mix well then set aside.

4 Add the remaining 10ml (2 tsp) olive oil to the non-stick frying pan that the potatoes and onions were cooked in. Set over a low–medium heat, then add the egg mixture into the pan, making sure the pan is evenly covered with the mixture. Cook for about 5 minutes until the top is just starting to set, then flip out onto a plate. Slide the tortilla back into the pan, so that the top is now on the bottom of the pan, and cook for a further 5 minutes until cooked through.

5 Meanwhile, for the salad, add the olive oil and lemon juice to a large bowl, season with salt and pepper, and whisk well. Add the spinach, rocket, dill, and chives, then toss everything together.

6 Slice up the tortilla, and serve with the salad.

Keep it This tortilla will keep well in the fridge for up to 4 days.

> Eggs are a great source of protein and vitamin B12, while the olive oil and slow-cooked onions bring the heart-healthy unsaturated fats and deep flavours that define this way of eating.

Tuna Niçoise Salad

Kcals 395
Protein 21g
Fibre 5g
Saturated Fat 3.8g
Unsaturated Fat 18.2g

Serves 2

Prep + cook time:
20 minutes

- ¼ red onion, thinly sliced
- 2 tbsp red wine vinegar
- 2 tsp maple syrup
- 200g (7oz) baby new potatoes, halved
- 100g (3½oz) green beans, trimmed
- 1 tsp Dijon mustard
- 40ml (2½ tbsp) extra virgin olive oil
- large handful of mixed salad leaves
- 1 large tomato, roughly chopped
- 1 tbsp capers
- 2 tbsp pitted green olives, chopped
- 1 x 145g (5oz) can tuna, drained
- handful of dill, chopped
- 1 tbsp dried oregano
- salt and freshly ground black pepper

1 Put the red onion into a small bowl and add 1 tablespoon red wine vinegar, 1 teaspoon maple syrup, and a pinch of salt. Scrunch together with your hands, then set aside to lightly pickle.

2 Fill a large saucepan with water, then set over a high heat. Once boiling, add the potatoes and cook for 12 minutes. Then, add the green beans and cook for a further 2 minutes, until both the potatoes and green beans are tender. Drain, then set aside to cool slightly.

3 Meanwhile, to a small bowl add the remaining 1 tablespoon red wine vinegar and 1 teaspoon maple syrup, along with the Dijon mustard and olive oil. Season with salt and freshly ground black pepper, whisk until you have a thick but pourable dressing, then set aside.

4 To a large bowl, add the salad leaves, tomatoes, capers, olives, tuna, green beans, and potatoes. Drizzle over the dressing and toss everything together. Top with the pickled red onion, dill, and oregano.

Tip You can cook the green beans and potatoes up to 2 days before assembling – just keep in the fridge until ready to serve.

This classic Mediterranean dish is rich in protein, omega-3 fats, and vitamin B12.

NUTRITIOUS LUNCHES

Halloumi Wraps

Kcals 629
Protein 35g
Fibre 7.4g
Saturated Fat 22g
Unsaturated Fat 15g

Serves 4

Prep + cook time: 15 minutes

- 1 red onion, thinly sliced
- juice of 1 lemon
- 2 tbsp extra virgin olive oil
- 2 x 225g (8oz) blocks of halloumi, cut into 2cm (¾in) slices
- 4 large wholemeal tortilla wraps
- 100g (scant ½ cup) tzatziki (see p148) or hummus
- 2 Little Gem lettuces, roughly chopped
- 3 tbsp pomegranate seeds
- small bunch of mint, roughly chopped
- salt

1 To a small bowl, add the red onion and lemon juice. Season with a pinch of salt, then scrunch together with your hands and set aside to pickle.

2 Add the olive oil to a frying pan set over a medium heat. Once hot, add the halloumi slices and fry for about 3 minutes on each side until golden in colour. Remove the slices from the pan and set aside.

3 Toast the tortilla wraps in the same pan or heat in a microwave.

4 To build the wraps, spread over some tzatziki or hummus, then top with the halloumi slices, lettuce, pomegranate seeds, chopped mint, and pickled red onion.

Swap it Make these wraps vegan by replacing the halloumi with some roasted courgette, and using hummus instead of tzatziki.

This quick lunch ticks the protein box with the halloumi and dip combo, as well as providing a good dose of wholegrain fibre from the wraps, and antioxidants from the salad accompaniments.

Cauliflower Salad Bowl

Kcals 448
Protein 14g
Fibre 6.7g
Saturated Fat 5g
Unsaturated Fat 23g

Serves 4

Prep + cook time:
30 minutes

- 1 small cauliflower, cut into small florets, plus cauliflower leaves
- 1 small aubergine, cut into 3cm (1¼in) chunks
- 1 courgette, cut into 3cm (1¼in) chunks
- 4 cloves of garlic, unpeeled
- 2 tbsp ras-el-hanout
- 3 tbsp extra virgin olive oil
- 200g (scant 1 cup) Greek yogurt
- grated zest and juice of 1 lemon
- 1 tbsp tahini
- 1 x 250g (9oz) pouch of microwaveable quinoa
- salt and freshly ground black pepper

1 Preheat the oven to 200°C (180°C fan/400°F/Gas 6).

2 To a large baking tray add the cauliflower and its leaves, the aubergine, courgette, and garlic. Sprinkle over the ras-el-hanout, then drizzle over the olive oil and season with salt and freshly ground black pepper. Mix well, then put into the oven and cook for 20 minutes until the vegetables are tender.

3 Meanwhile to a small bowl, add the yogurt, lemon zest, lemon juice, tahini, and a pinch of salt. Mix well, then set aside.

4 Heat the quinoa according to the packet instructions, then stir the quiona into the tray of cooked vegetables.

5 Divide the quinoa and vegetables among bowls, then top with the tahini yogurt and serve.

Keep it The quinoa and vegetables will keep in the fridge for 3 days. Just keep the yogurt dressing separate until ready to serve.

Roasted veg, grains, and a yogurt-tahini drizzle – this bowl is full of fibre, plant variety, and healthy fats to keep you feeling full.

NUTRITIOUS LUNCHES

Flatbread Pizza

Kcals 787
Protein 32g
Fibre 9.7g
Saturated Fat 16g
Unsaturated Fat 31g

Serves 4

Prep + cook time:
40 minutes

300g (2¼ cups) plain or wholemeal flour
2 tbsp extra virgin olive oil
½ tsp salt
120–150ml (½–⅔ cup) lukewarm water

Pesto:
3 tbsp pine nuts or walnuts
large handful of basil
½ clove of garlic, crushed
grated zest and juice of 1 lemon
60ml (¼ cup) extra virgin olive oil
2 tbsp finely grated Parmesan
salt and freshly ground black pepper

Toppings:
100ml (6½ tbsp) passata
1 red onion, thinly sliced
100g (1 cup) pitted black olives
100g (3½oz) Parma ham
250g (9oz) mozzarella
basil leaves

1 Add the flour, oil, and salt to a bowl. Slowly add the water, starting with 120ml (½ cup). Start to bring the dough together with your hands, adding more water if the mixture looks too dry. Knead until you have a smooth ball, then cover with cling film or a damp tea towel. Set aside.

2 For the pesto, lightly toast the pine nuts in a dry frying pan, then add to a blender with the basil, garlic, lemon zest, lemon juice, and Parmesan. Season with salt and freshly ground black pepper, then blitz until combined. Set aside.

3 Divide the dough into 4 pieces. Set a frying pan over a medium-high heat and preheat the grill.

4 Roll a piece of dough out to 1cm (½in) thick. Add it to the frying pan and cook for 2 minutes on each side, then transfer to a large baking tray and cover with a tea towel to keep warm. Repeat this for the remaining 3 portions of dough.

5 Top the flatbreads with the combination of toppings you prefer, then set the tray under the grill for 2 minutes until the cheese has melted. Top with the pesto and serve.

Using wholemeal flour here gives you 1 of your daily 2–3 servings of wholegrains.

Garlic Butter Prawns

Kcals 465
Protein 24g
Fibre 4g
Saturated Fat 14g
Unsaturated Fat 9g

Serves 2

Prep + cook time: 5 minutes

- 50g (3½ tbsp) butter
- ½ tsp chilli flakes
- 2 cloves of garlic, thinly sliced
- 165g (6oz) raw king prawns
- handful of parsley, chopped
- grated zest of 1 lemon
- ½ tsp smoked paprika
- salt and freshly ground black pepper

To serve (optional):
- a few slices of baguette

1 Add the butter to a frying pan set over a medium heat. Once melted, add the chilli flakes, garlic, and prawns. Cook for 3-4 minutes until the prawns turn pink, then remove from the heat.

2 Sprinkle over the parsley, lemon zest, and paprika. Season with a little salt and freshly ground black pepper and serve with the baguette slices for dipping.

Serve it This dish is perfect as part of a tapas feast - incredibly simple, yet so impressive!

Prawns provide lean protein, selenium, and vitamin B12, while garlic and parsley bring antioxidants and Mediterranean depth. Served with crusty bread, this is a quick and nourishing way to elevate lunch.

Roasted Potato Salad

Kcals	330
Protein	6.5g
Fibre	4.6g
Saturated Fat	4g
Unsaturated Fat	12g

Serves 4

Prep + cook time:
45 minutes

- 600g (1lb 5oz) new potatoes
- 3 tbsp extra virgin olive oil, plus extra for greasing
- 1 courgette, sliced
- 200g (scant 1 cup) natural yogurt
- grated zest and juice of 1 lemon
- handful of dill, roughly chopped
- handful of basil, roughly chopped
- 250g (9oz) jarred red peppers, thinly sliced
- 100g (1 cup) pitted black olives
- salt and freshly ground black pepper

1 Preheat the oven to 210°C (190° fan/425°F/Gas 7).

2 Fill a large saucepan with water and bring to the boil. Once boiling add the potatoes, then cook for 10–15 minutes until softened. Drain.

3 Grease a baking tray with oil, then arrange the potatoes on the baking tray. Flatten them down with the back of a large spoon, the drizzle over 2 tablespoons olive oil. Put the tray into the oven and cook for 15 minutes until the potatoes start to turn golden in colour.

4 Add the courgette slices to the tray, then drizzle over the remaining 1 tablespoon olive oil. Put the tray back into the oven and cook for a further 10–15 minutes until the potatoes are crispy and the courgettes have softened.

5 Meanwhile, to a large bowl, add the yogurt, lemon zest, lemon juice, dill, and basil. Season with salt and freshly ground black pepper, mix well, and set aside.

6 Add the potatoes and courgettes to the bowl, then add the peppers and olives. Toss everything together with the dressing and serve.

Serve it This salad works well on its own or with some simply cooked steak or fish.

New potatoes in their skins give a fibre boost to this dish, with the yogurt dressing adding extra protein and live cultures. Olives and herbs bring the Mediterranean flavours to this hearty salad.

NUTRITIOUS LUNCHES

Spanish-style Fish Stew

Kcals 395
Protein 29g
Fibre 3g
Saturated Fat 3g
Unsaturated Fat 24g

Serves 2

Prep + cook time: 20 minutes

- 1 tbsp extra virgin olive oil
- 1 banana/echalion shallot, finely chopped
- 3 cloves of garlic, crushed
- 1 tsp fennel seeds
- 400g (14oz) can chopped tomatoes
- pinch of saffron
- 250g (9oz) mussels, scrubbed clean and debearded
- 100g (3½oz) piece of cod, cut into 4cm (1½in) chunks
- 4 raw king prawns
- 2 tbsp mayonnaise
- 1 tsp Dijon mustard
- handful of parsley
- salt and freshly ground black pepper

To serve (optional):
baguette slices
lemon wedges

1 Add the olive oil to a high-sided frying pan set over a low-medium heat. Add the shallot and cook for 5 minutes until softened. Add in the garlic and fennel seeds, then cook for a further 2 minutes until fragrant.

2 Add in the chopped tomatoes, saffron, and mussels. Season with salt and freshly ground black pepper, then cover the pan with a lid and cook for 3 minutes.

3 Add in the cod and prawns, then cover and cook for a further 4 minutes until the mussel shells are fully open and the cod and prawns are cooked through. Discard any mussels that have not opened.

4 Meanwhile, to a small bowl add the mayonnaise and Dijon mustard, then mix and set aside.

5 Sprinkle the parsley over the fish stew and serve it with the mayonnaise, baguette slices, and lemon wedges.

Swap it This fish stew can be made just with the prawns, the cod, or the mussels, depending on what you have to hand. Just adjust the timings to suit.

This dish is rich in protein from lean white fish, as well as fibre and antioxidants from the tomatoes and olive oil.

Tabbouleh Salad

Kcals	192
Protein	1.3g
Fibre	1.2g
Saturated Fat	3g
Unsaturated Fat	13g

Serves 4

Prep + cook time: 25 minutes

- 30g (3 tbsp) bulgur wheat
- 60ml (¼ cup) boiling water
- large bunch of parsley, finely chopped
- small bunch of mint, finely chopped
- 1 large tomato, deseeded and finely chopped
- ½ red onion, finely chopped
- juice of 2 lemons
- 70ml (5 tbsp) extra virgin olive oil
- salt and freshly ground black pepper

1 Put the bulgur wheat into a small bowl, top with the boiling water, cover with cling film, and set aside for 20 minutes.

2 Meanwhile, add the parsley, mint, tomato, red onion, lemon juice, and olive oil to a bowl. Season with salt and freshly ground black pepper.

3 Fluff the bulgur wheat with a fork, then add to the bowl, mix through, and serve.

Serve it This is a fresh and delicious salad which can be enjoyed on its own, or as part of a bigger spread. Serve it alongside some simply cooked fish or grilled chicken.

Packed with herbs, wholegrains, and vitamin C, this salad is a fresh, flavourful way to support digestion and energy – and a reminder that simple really can be enough.

Lemony Borlotti Bean Broth

Kcals 316
Protein 17g
Fibre 17g
Saturated Fat 2g
Unsaturated Fat 7g

Serves 2

Prep + cook time:
20 minutes

- 1 tbsp extra virgin olive oil
- ½ onion, finely chopped
- 2 cloves of garlic, crushed
- 1 small courgette, roughly chopped
- 400g (14oz) can borlotti beans, drained and rinsed
- 500ml (2 cups) vegetable stock
- 100g (3½oz) spinach
- juice of 2 lemons
- handful of dill
- handful of chives, finely chopped
- salt and freshly ground black pepper

1 Add the olive oil to a saucepan set over a low-medium heat. Add the onion and cook for 5 minutes until softened. Add the garlic and cook for a further 2 minutes until fragrant.

2 Add in the courgette, borlotti beans, and vegetable stock, then cook for 10 minutes until the courgette has softened.

3 Add in the spinach, cover, then cook for 1 minute until the spinach has just wilted.

4 Add the lemon juice, and season well with salt and freshly ground black pepper.

5 Divide between two bowls and top with the dill and chives.

Swap it Adapt the recipe to whatever is in your store cupboard and fridge. Butter beans or chickpeas would also work well here, and you could swap the courgette or spinach for kale.

Borlotti beans are packed with plant protein, fibre, and potassium. This is a light yet satisfying meal that supports gut health and energy.

NUTRITIOUS LUNCHES

Midweek Dinners

These tasty recipes are quick and easy to prepare in the evening, and will ensure you make healthy meal choices after a busy day. From a simple Seafood Paella or Spaghetti Vongole to Harissa Beef Meatballs or Mushroom Risotto, these meals are all simple yet satisfying.

Herby Couscous Stuffed Peppers

Kcals 261
Protein 7g
Fibre 7g
Saturated Fat 3g
Unsaturated Fat 8g

Serves 2

Prep + cook time:
30 minutes

- 50g (scant ⅓ cup) couscous
- juice of 1 lemon
- 2 peppers, halved and deseeded
- 1 tbsp extra virgin olive oil
- 1 large tomato, finely chopped
- handful of mint, roughly chopped
- handful of basil, roughly chopped
- handful of flat leaf parsley, roughly chopped
- handful of dill, roughly chopped
- ¼ red onion, finely chopped
- 2 tbsp pitted green olives, finely chopped
- 20g (¾oz) feta
- salt and freshly ground black pepper

1 Preheat the oven to 190°C (170°C fan/375°F/Gas 5).

2 Add the couscous to a bowl and pour over boiling water until just covered. Add the lemon juice, cover with cling film, and leave to sit for 10 minutes.

3 Meanwhile, put the pepper halves onto a baking tray, cut-side up. Drizzle over the olive oil, then put into the oven for 15 minutes until they have slightly softened.

4 Fluff up the couscous with a fork, then add the tomato, mint, basil, parsley, dill, red onion, and olives. Season with salt and freshly ground black pepper, then mix well.

5 Fill each of the pepper halves with the couscous mix, then put back into the oven for a further 10 minutes until the peppers are soft.

6 Crumble over the feta and serve.

Serve it These peppers would look fabulous as part of a Mediterranean feast!

Swap it To make these vegan, leave out the feta.

Peppers are full of polyphenols, vitamin C, and antioxidants, while the herby couscous filling leaves you feeling full up.

Caponata Pasta

Kcals 434
Protein 16g
Fibre 10g
Saturated Fat 4g
Unsaturated Fat 10g

Serves 4

**Prep + cook time:
35 minutes**

- 1 aubergine, cut into 3cm (1¼in) chunks
- 1 courgette, cut into 3cm (1¼in) chunks
- 100g (3½oz) cherry tomatoes
- 2 tbsp extra virgin olive oil
- 1 onion, finely chopped
- 3 cloves of garlic, crushed
- 1 tbsp tomato purée
- 50g (½ cup) pitted black olives, roughly chopped
- 1 tbsp capers
- 1 tbsp pine nuts or walnuts
- 2 tbsp red wine vinegar
- 1 tbsp caster sugar
- 300g (10½oz) wholewheat pasta
- 3 tbsp finely grated Parmesan
- salt and freshly ground black pepper

1 Preheat the oven to 200°C (180°C fan/400°F/Gas 6).

2 Arrange the aubergine, courgette, and tomatoes on a large baking tray. Drizzle over 1 tablespoon olive oil, then season with salt and freshly ground black pepper. Put into the oven and cook for 25 minutes until the vegetables have softened.

3 Meanwhile, fill a large saucepan with water and bring to the boil.

4 Add the remaining 1 tablespoon olive oil to a deep frying pan set over a low-medium heat. Add the onion and garlic and cook for 10 minutes until softened. Add the tomato purée, olives, capers, and pine nuts or walnuts. Cook for 5 minutes until the pine nuts or walnuts have toasted.

5 Salt the pan of boiling water, then add the pasta and cook according to the packet instructions.

6 Add the aubergine, courgette, and tomatoes into the frying pan, then add the red wine vinegar and sugar. Season with salt and freshly ground black pepper and cook for a further few minutes.

7 Reserve a cup of the pasta water, then drain the pasta and add it in to the frying pan. Add a little of the reserved pasta water, mixing until you have a sauce. Toss through the Parmesan and serve.

Keep it The sauce can be doubled up and kept in the fridge for up to 4 days, or frozen for up to 3 months.

Roasted veg, olives, and capers bring fibre and antioxidants, while the pasta and pine nuts add satisfaction. It's a great way to get in extra veg without overthinking it.

MIDWEEK DINNERS

Lemon & Garlic Chicken Traybake

Kcals 753
Protein 48g
Fibre 7g
Saturated Fat 10g
Unsaturated Fat 33g

Serves 4

Prep + cook time:
1 hour

- 800g (1¾lb) new potatoes, halved
- 2 lemons, 1 sliced, 1 juiced
- 2 sprigs of rosemary
- 6 cloves of garlic, unpeeled
- 1 tbsp fennel seeds
- 2 tbsp capers
- 100g (1 cup) pitted green olives
- 1 red onion, cut in small wedges
- 2 tbsp extra virgin olive oil
- 8 skin-on, bone-in chicken thighs
- 100g (3½oz) green beans, halved
- 2 tbsp honey
- handful of parsley, roughly chopped
- salt and freshly ground black pepper

1 Preheat the oven to 200°C (180°C fan/400°F/Gas 6).

2 To a large baking dish add the potatoes, lemon slices, rosemary, garlic, fennel seeds, capers, olives, and red onion. Drizzle over the olive oil, then top with the chicken thighs, skin-side up. Season with salt and freshly ground black pepper, then put into the oven and cook for 45 minutes.

3 Remove from the oven, then remove the chicken from the dish and set aside to rest.

4 Add the green beans to the dish, drizzle over the honey, and squeeze in the lemon juice. Mix well, then put back into the oven for 10 minutes.

5 Remove from the oven, squeeze the garlic out of the skins and mix well.

6 Sprinkle over the parsley, then add the chicken to the top to serve.

Swap it This would also work well with salmon; just top the dish with the fish for the final 10 minutes of cooking.

Tip To reduce the fat content, you could use skinless chicken thighs.

> Protein from the chicken, fibre from the beans and olives, and plenty of Mediterranean flavour from the herbs and veg – this one-tray dinner ticks every box.

MIDWEEK DINNERS

Pissaladière

Kcals 371
Protein 9g
Fibre 3g
Saturated Fat 10g
Unsaturated Fat 16g

Serves 6

Prep + cook time:
1 hour

- 2 tbsp extra virgin olive oil
- 15g (1 tbsp) unsalted butter
- 3 large onions, thinly sliced
- 2 bay leaves
- 320g (11oz) puff pastry sheet
- 100g (3½oz) anchovy fillets
- 150g (1½ cups) pitted black olives
- 1 small egg
- salt and freshly ground black pepper

1 Add the olive oil and butter to a large saucepan set over a low-medium heat. Add the onions and bay leaves, season with salt and freshly ground black pepper, then cook for about 30 minutes, stirring regularly, until golden and caramelized. Set aside to cool slightly.

2 Preheat the oven to 200°C (180°C fan/400°F/Gas 6).

3 Lay the pastry sheet onto a baking sheet, and spread the onions over it, leaving a 2cm (¾in) border. Arrange the anchovy fillets on top in a criss-cross pattern. Add the olives into the spaces.

4 Crack the egg into a small bowl, whisk well, then brush onto the pastry border.

5 Put into the oven and bake for 25 minutes until the pastry is golden.

Serve it This would work well served with a simple green salad, or as part of a bigger spread.

Anchovies and olives provide key omega-3s and monounsaturated fats. Add caramelized onions for extra flavour and you've got a dish that's got substance.

Mushroom Risotto

Kcals 465
Protein 17g
Fibre 4g
Saturated Fat 7g
Unsaturated Fat 10g

Serves 4

Prep + cook time:
45 minutes

- 35g (1¼oz) dried porcini mushrooms
- 100ml (6½ tbsp) boiling water
- 2 tbsp extra virgin olive oil
- 1 banana/echalion shallot, finely chopped
- 300g (generous 1½ cups) risotto rice
- 200g (7oz) chestnut mushrooms, sliced
- 1 litre (4 cups) hot vegetable stock
- 4 sprigs of thyme, leaves picked
- grated zest and juice of 1 lemon
- 30g (scant ½ cup) finely grated Parmesan
- 30g (2 tbsp) unsalted butter
- handful of parsley, roughly chopped
- salt and freshly ground black pepper

1 Soak the porcini mushrooms in the boiling water for 20 minutes.

2 Meanwhile, add the olive oil to a large saucepan set over a low-medium heat. Once hot, add the shallot, and cook for 5 minutes until softened. Add the risotto rice, and cook for 3 minutes until lightly toasted. Add the chestnut mushrooms, then cook for 5 minutes until golden in colour.

3 Add the porcini mushrooms, along with the soaking liquid, then add the vegetable stock, a little at a time, stirring regularly, for about 25 minutes until the rice has absorbed all of the liquid and is cooked through.

4 Add the thyme, lemon zest, lemon juice, Parmesan, butter, and parsley. Season with salt and freshly ground black pepper, and serve.

Swap it Use whatever mushrooms you can find in your supermarket. Shiitake mushrooms would also work well here.

Mushrooms bring with them B vitamins, selenium, and fibre to support immune and gut health.

MIDWEEK DINNERS

Spiced Butternut Squash Tagine

Kcals 392
Protein 13g
Fibre 14g
Saturated Fat 2g
Unsaturated Fat 11g

Serves 4

Prep + cook time:
40 minutes

- 2 tbsp extra virgin olive oil
- 2 onions, grated
- 4 cloves of garlic, crushed
- 2 tbsp harissa
- 1 tsp ground cumin
- 1 tsp ground turmeric
- 1 butternut squash, peeled and cut into 4cm (1½in) chunks
- 1 courgette, cut into 4cm (1½in) chunks
- 400g (14oz) can chickpeas, drained and rinsed
- 70g (generous ⅔ cup) pitted green olives, roughly chopped
- 50g (1¾oz) dried apricots, roughly chopped
- 400g (14oz) can chopped tomatoes
- 500ml (2 cups) vegetable or chicken stock
- handful of parsley or coriander, chopped
- juice of 1 lemon
- salt and freshly ground black pepper

1 Add the olive oil to a large saucepan set over a low-medium heat. Add the onion and garlic, then cook for 10 minutes until the onion has softened.

2 Add the harissa, cumin, and turmeric, then cook for 1 minute until fragrant.

3 Add the butternut squash, courgette, chickpeas, olives, apricots, chopped tomatoes, and stock. Season with salt and pepper, stir well, then cover with a lid and cook for about 20 minutes until the vegetables are tender.

4 Add the parsley or coriander and lemon juice, then serve.

Keep it This would keep well in the fridge for up to 5 days, and freeze for up to 3 months.

This plant-powered dish is rich in fibre, antioxidants, and polyphenols. The squash, chickpeas, and olives combine to bring regulation to blood sugar.

Harissa Salmon

Kcals	559
Protein	28g
Fibre	6g
Saturated Fat	5g
Unsaturated Fat	23g

Serves 4

Prep + cook time:
30 minutes

- 200g (7oz) green beans, trimmed
- 200g (7oz) bulgur wheat
- 4 fillets of salmon
- 2 tbsp harissa
- 3 tbsp extra virgin olive oil
- 1 clove of garlic, crushed
- 1 tsp honey
- juice of 2 lemons
- handful of coriander, roughly chopped
- salt and freshly ground black pepper

To serve:
lemon wedges

1 Fill a saucepan with 400ml (1¾ cups) water, add some salt, and bring to the boil.

2 Meanwhile, preheat the oven to 190°C (170°C fan/375°F/Gas 5).

3 Once the water is boiling, add the green beans and cook for 2 minutes. Remove with a slotted spoon and set aside. Keep the pan on the boil.

4 Add the bulgur wheat to the boiling water, then reduce to the lowest heat, cover with a lid, and cook for 12 minutes.

5 Meanwhile, put the salmon on a baking tray, skin-side down, and set aside.

6 To a small bowl, add the harissa, 2 tablespoons olive oil, the garlic, and honey. Spread the mix over the salmon, then season with salt and freshly ground black pepper. Put into the oven and cook for 12 minutes until the salmon is cooked through but still a coral-pink colour.

7 Remove the cooked bulgur from the heat and leave to stand, untouched, for 5 minutes.

8 Add the remaining 1 tablespoon olive oil to the bulgur, along with the lemon juice, and coriander. Season with salt and freshly ground black pepper and fluff up with a fork. Serve alongside the salmon and green beans, with lemon wedges.

Swap it Cod or sea bass would work well here.

Rich in omega-3 fats and protein, salmon supports brain and heart health. With wholegrain bulgur and fibrous greens, this is a balanced, anti-inflammatory dinner.

Steamed Sea Bass with Potatoes

Kcals	461
Protein	33g
Fibre	4g
Saturated Fat	6g
Unsaturated Fat	17g

Serves 2

Prep + cook time:
25 minutes

- 400g (14oz) new potatoes, halved
- handful of chives, finely chopped
- 10g (2 tsp) unsalted butter
- 2 sea bass fillets
- ½ orange, thinly sliced
- 1 lemon, thinly sliced
- 2 sprigs of rosemary
- 40g (generous ⅓ cup) pitted black olives
- 1 tbsp capers
- 2 tbsp extra virgin olive oil
- salt and freshly ground black pepper

Mustard mayo:
- 100g (7 tbsp) mayonnaise
- 1 tbsp Dijon mustard

1 Preheat the oven to 190°C (170°C fan/375°F/Gas 5).

2 Fill a large saucepan with water, then set over a high heat. Once the water is boiling, add the potatoes and cook for 15 minutes until softened. Drain the potatoes, return to the saucepan, then add the chives and butter. Season with salt and pepper, then mix well and set aside.

3 Meanwhile, place a piece of baking parchment onto a large baking sheet, then put the sea bass fillets onto the paper. Top the fish with the orange slices, lemon slices, rosemary, black olives, and capers. Season with salt and freshly ground black pepper, then drizzle over the olive oil. Bring the two long edges of the baking parchment together, then fold over several times to seal like a parcel, doing the same with the two short edges.

4 Put the baking tray into the oven and cook for 10 minutes until the fish is opaque.

5 To a small bowl, add the mayo and Dijon mustard, then mix well and set aside.

6 Unravel the parcel, then serve with the potatoes and mustard mayo on the side.

Tip The fish parcels can be assembled and kept in the fridge until you are ready to cook.

Sea bass provides lean protein and olive oil adds heart-healthy fats to this simple, yet delicious meal.

Marbella Chicken

Kcals 471
Protein 24g
Fibre 2g
Saturated Fat 6g
Unsaturated Fat 21g

Serves 4

Prep + cook time:
1 hour, plus marinating time

- 4 skin-on chicken leg portions
- 2 tbsp extra virgin olive oil
- 4 cloves of garlic, crushed
- small handful of fresh oregano, leaves picked
- 100g (1 cup) pitted green or black olives
- 80g (generous ½ cup) pitted prunes, roughly chopped
- 3 tbsp capers
- 60ml (¼ cup) red wine vinegar
- 3 tbsp soft light brown sugar
- 50g (1¾oz) red grapes
- 150ml (⅔ cup) white wine
- handful of basil
- salt and freshly ground black pepper

To serve (optional):
giant couscous

1 Add the chicken, olive oil, garlic, oregano, olives, prunes, capers, and red wine vinegar to a large zip-lock bag. Season with salt and freshly ground black pepper, then leave to marinate in the fridge for a few hours, or overnight.

2 When ready to cook, preheat the oven to 190°C (170°C fan/375°F/Gas 5).

3 Spread the contents of the bag into a large baking dish in a single layer with the chicken skin-side up. Sprinkle over the sugar, then top with the grapes. Pour the white wine into the dish, then season with salt and freshly ground black pepper. Cook for 50 minutes until the chicken is cooked through.

4 Scatter over the basil, and serve with giant couscous, if liked.

> Olives, capers, and prunes are rich in polyphenols that support heart and gut health. Paired with protein-rich chicken and a splash of red wine vinegar, this dish is full of flavour and Mediterranean goodness.

Turkey Kebabs

Kcals 422
Protein 39g
Fibre 6g
Saturated Fat 3g
Unsaturated Fat 5g

Serves 4

Prep + cook time:
20 minutes

500g (1lb 2oz) turkey mince
1 tbsp ground cumin
1 tsp allspice
½ tsp ground turmeric
1 tsp ground coriander
½ tsp cayenne pepper
¼ red onion, finely chopped
handful of parsley, roughly chopped
4 wholemeal flatbreads
1 Little Gem lettuce, shredded
3 tbsp tzatziki
1 large tomato, cut into wedges
¼ cucumber, cut into strips
extra virgin olive oil spray
salt and freshly ground black pepper

1 To a large bowl, add the turkey mince, cumin, allspice, turmeric, ground coriander, cayenne pepper, red onion, and parsley. Season with salt and freshly ground black pepper, then mix well.

2 Roll the mix into 12 kofta shapes. If you have skewers, skewer the koftas; if not shape them with your hands. Put them onto a baking tray and set aside.

3 Preheat the grill.

4 Spray the koftas with some oil and set the tray under the grill. Cook for 4 minutes on each side until golden in colour and cooked through.

5 Meanwhile, heat the flatbreads in a frying pan or microwave.

6 Serve the flatbreads with the koftas, lettuce, tzatziki, tomato, and cucumber.

Swap it You could also use beef or lamb mince here.

Lean turkey offers a lower-fat source of protein, combined with wholegrain flatbreads and a calcium and/or fibre boost from the accompaniments – this is a well-rounded dish.

Cheesy Polenta with Mushrooms

Kcals 305
Protein 20g
Fibre 11g
Saturated Fat 6g
Unsaturated Fat 7g

Serves 4

Prep + cook time:
35 minutes

- 30g (1oz) dried porcini mushrooms
- 80ml (⅓ cup) boiling water
- 600ml (2½ cups) vegetable stock
- 100g (⅔ cup) polenta
- 20g (1½ tbsp) butter
- 3 tbsp finely grated Parmesan, plus extra to serve
- 1 tbsp extra virgin olive oil
- 400g (14oz) shiitake, oyster, or chestnut mushrooms, thinly sliced
- 3 tbsp miso paste
- 3 tbsp soy sauce
- 1 tbsp maple syrup
- pinch of chilli flakes
- handful of parsley, roughly chopped
- salt and freshly ground black pepper

1 Add the dried porcini mushrooms to a measuring jug, then pour the boiling water over, and leave to soak for 10 minutes. Drain the mushrooms, reserving their soaking liquid. Roughly chop the mushrooms, then set aside.

2 Add the vegetable stock to a saucepan and bring to the boil. Once boiling, reduce to a low heat, then add in the polenta. Whisk continuously for 20–25 minutes until the polenta is tender and has absorbed the liquid. Add the butter and Parmesan, season generously with salt and freshly ground black pepper, then mix well.

3 Meanwhile, add the olive oil to a large frying pan set over a high heat. Once hot, add the fresh mushrooms. Season with salt and freshly ground black pepper, and cook for 5 minutes until golden.

4 Add in the miso paste, soy, maple syrup, chilli flakes, porcini mushrooms, and the reserved porcini liquid, and 2 tablespoons water. Cook for a further 3 minutes until the sauce has thickened, then set aside.

5 Divide the polenta among plates, top with the mushrooms, then sprinkle over the parsley, extra grated Parmesan, and some black pepper.

Swap it To make this vegan, leave out the Parmesan and replace the butter with margarine.

Polenta is a gluten-free source of slow-release carbs.

MIDWEEK DINNERS

Harissa Beef Meatballs

Kcals 591
Protein 51g
Fibre 9g
Saturated Fat 6g
Unsaturated Fat 13g

Serves 4

Prep + cook time: 40 minutes

- 1 tbsp extra virgin olive oil
- 2 cloves of garlic, thinly sliced
- 2 x 400g (14oz) cans chopped tomatoes
- 2 tbsp harissa
- 400g (14oz) beef mince
- 200g (7oz) pork mince
- 1 tsp ground cinnamon
- 1 tsp paprika
- 1 tsp ground cumin
- 1 tsp dried oregano, plus extra to serve
- 1 small red onion, grated
- 1 small egg
- 50g (1 cup) fresh breadcrumbs
- 2 x 250g (9oz) pouches of microwaveable Mediterranean grains
- handful of parsley, roughly chopped
- salt and freshly ground black pepper

1 Add the olive oil to a frying pan set over a low-medium heat. Once hot, add the garlic and cook for 1 minute until fragrant. Add the chopped tomatoes and 1 tablespoon harissa. Season with salt and freshly ground black pepper, then cook for 10–15 minutes until slightly reduced.

2 Meanwhile, add the remaining 1 tablespoon harissa to a bowl with the beef mince, pork mince, cinnamon, paprika, cumin, oregano, onion, egg, and breadcrumbs. Season with salt and freshly ground black pepper, then shape into 16 balls.

3 Add the meatballs to the tomato sauce and cook for 20 minutes, turning regularly, until cooked through.

4 Heat the microwaveable grains according to the packet instructions.

5 Sprinkle the parsley over the meatballs, top with some dried oregano, and serve with the grains on the side.

Swap it These meatballs would also work well with lamb mince.

These meatballs offer protein, iron, and zinc, while the sauce boasts antioxidants.

Seafood Paella

Kcals 305
Protein 28g
Fibre 2g
Saturated Fat 2g
Unsaturated Fat 6g

Serves 4

Prep + cook time: 55 minutes

- 1 tbsp extra virgin olive oil
- 1 onion, finely chopped
- 1 red pepper, roughly chopped
- 2 cloves of garlic, thinly sliced
- 2 tomatoes, grated
- 1 tsp smoked paprika
- pinch of saffron (optional)
- 250g (1⅓ cups) paella rice
- 1 litre (4 cups) fish or chicken stock
- 2 cod fillets, cut into 4cm (1½in) chunks
- 165g (5oz) raw king prawns
- 200g (7oz) mussels or clams, scrubbed clean and debearded
- handful of parsley, roughly chopped
- salt and freshly ground black pepper

To serve:
lemon wedges

1 Add 1 tablespoon olive oil to a deep shallow casserole dish set over a low-medium heat. Once hot, add the onion, red pepper, and garlic, and cook for 10 minutes until softened.

2 Add the grated tomatoes, paprika, and saffron (if using), cook for 1 minute, then add the paella rice and stock. Bring to the boil, then reduce to a low simmer and cook, uncovered, for 25 minutes.

3 Add the cod chunks, prawns, and mussels or clams to the paella rice, season with salt and pepper, and cook for a further 5 minutes.

4 Cover with a lid, remove from the heat, and let it sit for 10 minutes until the mussels or clam shells are open. Discard any mussels or clams that have not opened.

5 Sprinkle over the parsley and serve with lemon wedges for squeezing.

Swap it Swap the cod for any other fish, or use only prawns, mussels, or clams, if preferred.

This vibrant dish is rich in lean protein from fish and shellfish, along with valuable selenium, iodine, and vitamin B12.

Spaghetti Vongole

Kcals 509
Protein 33g
Fibre 10g
Saturated Fat 5g
Unsaturated Fat 8g

Serves 3

**Prep + cook time:
20 minutes**

- 200g (7oz) dried spaghetti
- 1 tbsp extra virgin olive oil
- 1 banana/echalion shallot, finely chopped
- 1 large tomato, deseeded and finely chopped
- 1 red chilli, deseeded and finely chopped
- 20g (1½ tbsp) unsalted butter
- 20ml (4 tsp) white wine
- 500g (1lb 2oz) clams, scrubbed clean
- juice of 1 lemon
- handful of parsley, roughly chopped
- salt and freshly ground black pepper

1 Fill a large saucepan with water, then set over a high heat. Once boiling, add the pasta and cook according to the packet instructions.

2 Meanwhile, add the olive oil to high-sided frying pan, set over a low–medium heat. Add the shallot, tomato, and red chilli, then cook for 4 minutes until softened.

3 Add in the butter, white wine, and clams. Cover the pan with a lid and cook for 5 minutes, or until the clams have opened, discarding any that remain closed.

4 Reserve a cup of pasta water, drain the spaghetti, then add the spaghetti into the frying pan. Add the lemon juice and some of the pasta water. Season with salt and freshly ground black pepper, and mix well.

5 Sprinkle over the parsley and serve.

Swap it You can also use other shellfish, such as mussels or prawns.

Clams are a great source of iodine, vitamin B12, and iron. Combined with chilli, parsley, and olive oil, this dish feels both light and indulgent.

Batch Cooking & Meal Prep

Cooking in batches and prepping ahead is a great way to ensure you avoid making unhealthy and impulse-driven choices when you feel busy and tired. Not only does it save time and mental energy, but it also helps you to stay focused on your goals, even on your busiest days.

Falafels

Kcals 281
Protein 16g
Fibre 13g
Saturated Fat 0g
Unsaturated Fat 5g

Serves 4

Prep + cook time:
30 minutes

2 x 400g (14oz) cans chickpeas, drained and rinsed
1 small onion, roughly chopped
2 cloves of garlic, roughly chopped
2 tsp ground cumin
2 tsp ground coriander
1 tsp cayenne pepper
handful of parsley, roughly chopped
1 tsp baking powder
1 tbsp chickpea flour
vegetable or olive oil spray
salt and freshly ground black pepper

To serve (optional):
pitta breads
hummus
sliced tomatoes
sliced cucumber
sliced red cabbage

1 Preheat the oven to 200°C (180°C fan/400°F/Gas 6) and line a large baking tray with baking parchment.

2 To a blender add the chickpeas, onion, garlic, cumin, coriander, cayenne pepper, parsley, baking powder, and chickpea flour. Season with salt and freshly ground black pepper, then blitz until the mixture is combined but has a coarse texture.

3 Shape into 12 balls, then put onto the lined baking tray. Spray liberally with oil, then cook for 20 minutes until golden.

4 Serve with pitta breads, hummus, tomato, cucumber, and red cabbage.

Keep it These will freeze well for up to 3 months.

> Chickpeas are a great source of plant-based protein, fibre, and prebiotics to support gut health. Baked, not fried, these falafels are a heart-friendly Mediterranean classic.

Greek Salad

Kcals	236
Protein	6g
Fibre	4g
Saturated Fat	6g
Unsaturated Fat	13g

Serves 4

Prep + cook time:
10 minutes

- 4 large tomatoes, roughly chopped
- 1 cucumber, roughly chopped
- ½ red onion, thinly sliced
- ½ green pepper, deseeded and roughly chopped
- 100g (1 cup) pitted black olives
- 1 tsp dried oregano
- 100g (3½oz) feta
- 3 tbsp extra virgin olive oil
- 1 tbsp red wine vinegar
- salt and freshly ground black pepper

1 To a bowl, add the tomatoes, cucumber, red onion, pepper, olives, and oregano. Break the feta into chunks, add to the bowl, and set aside.

2 To a small bowl, add the olive oil and red wine vinegar. Season with salt and freshly ground black pepper and whisk well.

3 Pour the dressing over the salad, mix well, and serve.

Keep it This salad will keep in the fridge for 4 days without the dressing.

> Crisp veg, olives, and feta bring a mix of fibre, healthy fats, and calcium to this salad. A simple way to boost your plant intake in this world-famous salad from the heart of the Med.

Spinach Fritters with Courgette Yogurt

Kcals 639
Protein 21g
Fibre 10g
Saturated Fat 8g
Unsaturated Fat 28g

Serves 4

Prep + cook time: 25 minutes

- 400g (14oz) spinach
- 150g (5¼oz) pouch of microwaveable bulgar wheat or quinoa
- 2 tsp ground cumin
- 2 cloves of garlic, crushed
- grated zest of 2 lemons
- 150g (5¼oz) sun-dried tomatoes, roughly chopped
- 100g (3½oz) feta
- 2 eggs
- 180g (3½ cups) fresh breadcrumbs
- 2 tbsp extra virgin olive oil
- salt and freshly ground black pepper
- salad leaves, to serve

Courgette yogurt:

- 1 small courgette, finely chopped
- grated zest and juice of 1 lemon
- 100g (scant ½ cup) Greek yogurt
- handful of dill, roughly chopped
- 1 red chilli, deseeded and finely chopped
- salt and freshly ground black pepper

1 Add the spinach to a colander and put in the sink. Pour boiling water from the kettle over the spinach until wilted. Once cool enough to handle, squeeze out as much water as possible.

2 Finely chop the spinach and put into a large bowl. Add the quinoa or bulgar wheat, cumin, garlic, lemon zest, sun-dried tomatoes, feta, eggs, and breadcrumbs, then season with salt and pepper. Shape the mixture into 12 patties.

3 Add the olive oil to a frying pan over a medium heat. Fry the patties for 4 minutes on each side until golden. You may need to do this in batches.

4 To a small bowl, add the courgette, lemon zest, lemon juice, yogurt, dill, and red chilli. Season with salt and pepper, then serve alongside the fritters. Serve with some leaves on the side.

Keep it These fritters can be kept in the fridge for 4 days or frozen for up to 3 months.

A brilliant way to use up greens and herbs, these fritters provide fibre, protein, and a mix of textures.

Focaccia

Kcals 349
Protein 10g
Fibre 3g
Saturated Fat 1g
Unsaturated Fat 6g

Serves 6

Prep + cook time:
35 minutes, plus resting time

500g (generous 3½ cups) strong bread flour
6g (2 tsp) instant dried yeast
11g (2 tsp) fine salt
400–440ml (1¾–scant 2 cups) lukewarm water
40ml (2 tbsp plus 2 tsp) extra virgin olive oil, plus extra for greasing

Toppings (optional):
flaky salt
pitted green olives
cherries or grapes
rosemary

1 To a very large bowl or container, add the flour, yeast, and salt. Add the water, starting with 400ml (1¾ cups), and mix with your hands until you have a shaggy dough and it looks quite wet. Add more water if it looks too dry.

2 Cover with cling film or a damp tea towel, and leave for 12–14 hours or overnight.

3 After it has rested, oil a cast-iron frying pan or deep baking tray and turn the dough out into the pan or tray. Drizzle over the olive oil and press dimples into the dough. Top with any of the toppings listed, or leave it plain. Cover again and leave for 2 hours.

4 Preheat the oven to 240°C (220°C fan/475°F/Gas 9).

5 Put the bread into the oven and cook for about 25 minutes until golden and cooked through.

Tip This focaccia recipe couldn't be easier! Make the night before, then when you wake up, your dough will be risen and ready for you.

A source of energizing carbohydrates and heart-healthy olive oil. Top with olives or herbs for a simple side that complements protein and veg-rich meals.

Stifado

Kcals	512
Protein	59g
Fibre	3g
Saturated Fat	7g
Unsaturated Fat	14g

Serves 4

Prep + cook time:
2 hours 30 minutes

- 2 tbsp extra virgin olive oil
- 1kg (2¼lb) stewing beef, cut into large chunks
- 4 banana/echalion shallots, halved
- 4 cloves of garlic, crushed
- 150ml (⅔ cup) red wine
- 500ml (2 cups) passata
- 1 cinnamon stick
- 200ml (scant 1 cup) beef stock
- 4 cloves
- 2 bay leaves
- ½ tsp allspice
- salt and freshly ground black pepper

To serve (optional):
- 2 x 250g (9oz) pouches of microwavable grains
- handful of parsley, finely chopped

1 Add the olive oil to a large flameproof casserole dish set over a high heat. Once hot, add the beef in batches and cook until deep brown in colour on all sides. Remove from the pan and set aside.

2 Reduce the heat to low, add the shallots and garlic to the pan, then cook for 2 minutes until softened. Add the red wine and let it bubble for a couple of minutes.

3 Add the passata, cinnamon stick, beef stock, cloves, bay leaves, and allspice, then return the beef to the pan. Season with salt and freshly ground black pepper, mix well, cover with a lid, and cook for around 2 hours until the beef is tender.

4 Serve with microwaved grains and a scattering of chopped parsley, if liked.

Keep it This will keep in the fridge for up to 3 days, or in the freezer for up to 3 months.

> Slow-cooked beef is a source of iron and protein, while red wine adds polyphenols like resveratrol, which may support heart and blood vessel health.

Aubergine Parmigiana

Kcals	460
Protein	17g
Fibre	8g
Saturated Fat	8g
Unsaturated Fat	12g

Serves 4

Prep + cook time:
1 hour 10 minutes

- 3 aubergines, cut lengthways into 2cm (¾in) slices
- 3 tbsp extra virgin olive oil
- 2 cloves of garlic, crushed
- 2 x 400g (14oz) cans chopped tomatoes
- handful of basil, roughly chopped
- 200g (2½ cups) dried breadcrumbs
- 40g (scant ⅔ cup) finely grated Parmesan
- 100g (1 cup) pre-grated mozzarella
- salt and freshly ground black pepper

1 Preheat the oven to 190°C (170°C fan/375°F/Gas 5).

2 Season the aubergine slices with salt and freshly ground black pepper, then set aside.

3 Add 2 tablespoons olive oil to a large frying pan, set over a high heat. Once hot, add the aubergine slices to the pan in a single layer, then fry for 3 minutes on either side until golden. Remove from the pan and set aside.

4 Add the remaining 1 tablespoon olive oil to a saucepan set over a low–medium heat. Once hot, add the garlic, then cook for 1 minute until fragrant. Add the chopped tomatoes and basil. Season with salt and freshly ground black pepper, then simmer gently for 20 minutes until reduced.

5 Layer the ingredients in a medium baking dish, starting with the tomatoes, followed by the breadcrumbs, Parmesan, and mozzarella, then a layer of aubergine slices, making sure they don't overlap. Repeat this process until you have used all the ingredients, finishing with breadcrumbs and cheese.

6 Put into the oven and cook for 35 minutes until bubbling.

Keep it This will keep in the fridge for up to 4 days, or in the freezer for up to 3 months.

Roasted aubergine layered with tomatoes and mozzarella makes this dish rich in fibre, antioxidants, and satisfaction.

Slow-cooked Lamb Shoulder

Kcals	699
Protein	41g
Fibre	4g
Saturated Fat	18g
Unsaturated Fat	26g

Serves 4–6

Prep + cook time: 4 hours

- 3 onions, 2 sliced into thick rounds, 1 finely chopped
- 2 heads of garlic, halved horizontally
- 1.5kg (3¼lb) bone-in shoulder of lamb
- 3 tbsp olive oil
- 2 tbsp ground cumin
- 1 tbsp ground coriander
- 1 tsp ground turmeric
- 1 tsp ground cinnamon
- 600ml (2½ cups) hot chicken stock
- 2 tomatoes, roughly chopped
- 1 tbsp tomato purée
- 200g (scant 1¼ cups) bulgar wheat
- salt and freshly ground black pepper

1 Preheat the oven to 220°C (200°C fan/425°F/Gas 7).

2 Arrange the onion rounds in a large baking dish, add the garlic, and top with the lamb, skin-side up. Brush the lamb with 1 tablespoon olive oil, then season with salt and pepper. Put into the oven and cook, uncovered, for 30 minutes.

3 Meanwhile, to a small bowl, add the cumin, coriander, turmeric, cinnamon, and 1 tablespoon olive oil. Season with salt, then mix to a paste.

4 Remove the lamb from the oven, then reduce the heat to 180°C (160°C fan/350°F/Gas 4). Brush the spice mix all over the lamb, then pour 200ml (scant 1 cup) chicken stock into the baking dish. Cover tightly with tin foil, then cook for 3 hours. When the lamb is cooked, let it sit, covered, for 30 minutes while you prepare the bulgar.

5 Add the remaining 1 tablespoon olive oil to a saucepan set over a low–medium heat. Add the chopped onion and cook for 5 minutes until softened. Add the tomatoes and tomato purée and cook for 3 minutes. Add the bulgar and the remaining chicken stock. Bring to the boil, reduce to a simmer, then cover and cook for 10 minutes.

6 Remove from the heat and let it sit, covered, for 10 minutes. Season, fluff with a fork, and serve with the rested lamb.

Lamb is full of iron, zinc, and high-quality protein, while the slow-cooked spices provide rich flavour and polyphenols.

Spinach Lasagne

Kcals	494
Protein	20g
Fibre	2g
Saturated Fat	12g
Unsaturated Fat	15g

Serves 6

Prep + cook time: 45 minutes

250g (9oz) spinach
50g (3½ tbsp) butter
50g (6 tbsp) plain flour
500ml (2 cups) skimmed milk
pinch of nutmeg
150g (¾ cup) pesto
250g (9oz) fresh lasagne sheets
200g (2 cups) pre-grated mozzarella
40g (scant ⅔ cup) finely grated Parmesan
salt and freshly ground black pepper

To serve (optional):
salad leaves

A comforting bake rich in calcium and iron from spinach, plus a good dose of protein and flavour from the creamy béchamel.

1 Preheat the oven to 190°C (170°C fan/375°F/Gas 5).

2 Put the spinach into a colander in the sink and pour boiling water over the spinach until just wilted. Once cool enough to handle, squeeze the water out of the spinach, then roughly chop and set aside.

3 Meanwhile, add the butter to a saucepan, set over a low-medium heat. Once the butter has melted, add the flour and whisk until it looks like a thick paste. Continue to cook for 30 seconds to cook out the flour. Add the milk, bit by bit, whisking continuously until it reaches the consistency of double cream. Add in the nutmeg, season with salt and freshly ground black pepper, then set aside.

4 To assemble the lasagne, spread a layer of the béchamel on the bottom of a large baking dish. Dot over some of the pesto, then sprinkle over some of the mozzarella, Parmesan, and chopped spinach. Add a layer of the lasagne sheets. In this order, repeat the process until everything is used up, finishing with béchamel and grated cheese on top.

5 Cook on the middle shelf of the oven for 35 minutes until bubbling. Serve with salad leaves, if you like.

Keep it This will keep in the fridge for up to 4 days, or in the freezer for 3 months.

Chicken Meatballs

Kcals 376
Protein 38g
Fibre 2g
Saturated Fat 3g
Unsaturated Fat 11g

Serves 4

Prep + cook time:
30 minutes

- 100g (2 cups) fresh breadcrumbs
- 3 tbsp milk
- 500g (1lb 2oz) chicken mince
- handful of mint, roughly chopped
- handful of parsley, roughly chopped
- handful basil, roughly chopped
- grated zest of 1 lemon
- 1 small red onion, finely chopped
- 2 tbsp extra virgin olive oil
- salt and freshly ground black pepper

To serve (optional):
- couscous
- tzatziki
- salad leaves
- sliced tomatoes
- lemon wedges

1 Add the breadcrumbs and milk to a bowl, mix, then set aside for 10 minutes.

2 Add the chicken mince, mint, parsley, basil, lemon zest, and onion to the bowl, then season with salt and freshly ground black pepper. Mix well, then shape into 16 meatballs and set aside.

3 Add the olive oil to a large frying pan set over a medium heat. Once hot, add the chicken meatballs in a single layer. Cook for about 10 minutes until cooked through and golden.

4 Serve with couscous, tzatziki, salad, and lemon wedges, if liked, for a speedy lunch.

Keep it These will keep in the freezer for up to 3 months.

This light meal option is packed with lean protein, herbs, and citrus for freshness.

Greens Filo Pie

Kcals 325
Protein 15g
Fibre 3g
Saturated Fat 9g
Unsaturated Fat 6g

Serves 6

Prep + cook time:
1 hour

- 1 tbsp extra virgin olive oil
- 1 onion, finely chopped
- 2 cloves of garlic, crushed
- 100g (3½oz) chard, stalks finely chopped and leaves roughly chopped
- 100g (3½oz) spinach
- 1 head of broccoli, cut into small florets
- 200g (7oz) feta
- 50g (¾ cup) grated Parmesan
- 2 large eggs
- grated zest of 2 lemons
- large handful of parsley, chopped
- handful of dill, chopped
- 30g (2 tbsp) butter, melted
- 270g (9½oz) pack of filo pastry
- salt and freshly ground black pepper

1 Add the olive oil to a large frying pan set over a low-medium heat. Add the onion, then cook for 5 minutes until softened. Add the garlic and cook for a further 5 minutes. Add the chard stalks and cook for 30 seconds before adding the chard leaves and spinach leaves. Pop on a lid and cook until the leaves have just wilted, then turn off the heat and set aside.

2 Preheat the oven to 190°C (170°C fan/375°F/Gas 5).

3 Cook the broccoli in a pan of boiling water for 1 minute, then drain and set aside.

4 To a large bowl, add the onion and spinach mixture and the broccoli. Crumble in the feta, add the Parmesan, eggs, lemon zest, parsley, and dill. Season well with salt and black pepper, mix together until fully combined, and set aside.

5 Brush a baking dish with a little melted butter, and lay a sheet of the filo into the dish. Brush with melted butter, and repeat to make 3 layers. Add the filling, then repeat the pastry and melted butter process with the remaining pastry on top.

6 Bake for 35 minutes until golden, and serve.

Keep it This pie will keep in the fridge for 5 days. Simply cut out a slice and reheat when needed.

Ratatouille

Kcals 159
Protein 4g
Fibre 5g
Saturated Fat 2g
Unsaturated Fat 8g

Serves 4

Prep + cook time:
1 hour

- 3 tbsp extra virgin olive oil
- 3 cloves of garlic, crushed
- 400g (14oz) can chopped tomatoes
- handful of basil, roughly chopped
- 2 courgettes, very thinly sliced
- 2 aubergines, very thinly sliced
- 2 tomatoes, very thinly sliced
- salt and freshly ground black pepper

1 Add 1 tablespoon olive oil to a shallow flameproof casserole dish set over a low–medium heat, add the garlic cloves, and cook for 1 minute. Add the chopped tomatoes, then turn up the heat and cook for 10 minutes until the sauce has reduced slightly. Season with salt and freshly ground black pepper, then stir through the basil and remove from the heat.

2 Preheat the oven to 200°C (180°C fan/400°F/Gas 6).

3 Arrange the sliced vegetables, in mini stacks, around the dish in a circular pattern on top of the cooked tomatoes.

4 Drizzle over the remaining 2 tablespoons olive oil, and season with salt and freshly ground black pepper.

5 Cook in the oven for 40 minutes until the vegetables are tender.

Keep it This will keep in the fridge for up to 4 days.

Slow-cooked veg like aubergine and courgette offer fibre and antioxidants. Cooking tomatoes boosts lycopene absorption, a heart-healthy antioxidant, especially when paired with olive oil and herbs.

Air Fryer & Slow Cooker

An air fryer can be a handy piece of kit when sticking to a Mediterranean diet – and can also produce some crispy treats, using much less oil than frying. A slow cooker is a convenient way to prepare meals. Simply add in the ingredients, and when you return hours later, you'll have something healthy and delicious waiting for you at the end of the day!

Chicken Gyros

Kcals 526
Protein 40g
Fibre 8g
Saturated Fat 5g
Unsaturated Fat 13g

Serves 4

Prep + cook time:
30 minutes, plus marinating time

- 4 chicken thighs
- 100g (scant ½ cup) Greek yogurt
- 1 tbsp extra virgin olive oil
- 1 tsp ground cumin
- 1 tsp ground coriander
- 1 tsp smoked paprika
- juice of 2 lemons
- 1 red onion
- 100g (3½oz) oven chips
- 100g (scant ½ cup) tzatziki (see p148)
- 4 flatbreads
- ¼ red cabbage, finely shredded
- 2 tomatoes, roughly chopped
- salt and freshly ground black pepper

1 To a large bowl, add the chicken thighs, Greek yogurt, olive oil, cumin, coriander, paprika, and the juice from 1 lemon. Season with salt and freshly ground black pepper, mix well, cover, and leave to marinate in the fridge for an hour, or overnight.

2 Meanwhile, to a small bowl add the red onion and the juice from the remaining lemon. Season with a little salt, then scrunch together with your hands and set aside to lightly pickle.

3 Preheat the air fryer to 200°C/400°F for 3 minutes.

4 Add the chips to the air fryer basket and cook according to the packet instructions. Set aside.

5 Add the marinated chicken to the air fryer basket and cook at 180°C/350°F for 15 minutes until charred and cooked through. If you have an air fryer with 2 drawers, you can cook the chips and chicken at the same time. Remove the bones from the chicken thighs, slice, then set aside.

6 Spread the tzatziki onto the flatbreads, top with the red cabbage, tomatoes, chicken, chips, and pickled onion, then serve.

Swap it Chicken breast would also work here.

> Marinated chicken and creamy tzatziki deliver protein and satisfaction here, while the fresh veg and lemony pickled onions add crunch and brightness.

AIR FRYER & SLOW COOKER

Chickpea & Halloumi Salad

Kcals 587
Protein 27g
Fibre 10g
Saturated Fat 13g
Unsaturated Fat 20g

Serves 2

Prep + cook time:
20 minutes

- 1 courgette, roughly chopped
- 1 red onion, cut into wedges
- 1 red pepper, roughly chopped
- 250g (9oz) pouch of microwaveable Mediterranean grains
- 400g (14oz) can chickpeas, drained and rinsed
- 250g (9oz) pack of halloumi, cut into 3cm (1¼in) slices
- juice of 1 lemon
- 1 tsp dried oregano
- 1 tsp honey
- 60ml (¼ cup) extra virgin olive oil
- 100g (3½oz) rocket
- handful of basil
- vegetable or olive oil spray
- salt and freshly ground black pepper

1 Preheat the air fryer to 180°C/350°F for 3 minutes.

2 To the air fryer basket, add the courgette, red onion, and red pepper. Spray with some oil, then cook at 180°C/350°F for 8 minutes until the vegetables are tender and charred in places. Remove from the air fryer and set aside.

3 Add the grains and chickpeas into the base of the air fryer, then spray with a little oil. Add the halloumi to the air fryer basket, then spray with a bit more of the oil. Put the basket into the air fryer and cook at 180°C/350°F for 7 minutes until the halloumi is golden and the grains and chickpeas are crispy.

4 Meanwhile, to a large bowl, add the lemon juice, oregano, honey, and extra virgin olive oil. Season with salt and freshly ground black pepper, then whisk well. Add the rocket, basil, vegetables, halloumi, grains, and chickpeas. Mix together well, and serve.

Swap it To make this vegan, leave out the halloumi and use maple syrup rather than honey.

This balanced bowl boasts fibre-rich chickpeas, protein from halloumi, and antioxidants from the veggies.

Baked Sweet Potatoes

Kcals 440
Protein 13g
Fibre 11g
Saturated Fat 2g
Unsaturated Fat 11g

Serves 4

Prep + cook time: 40 minutes

- 4 sweet potatoes
- 3 tbsp olive oil
- 400g (14oz) can green lentils, drained and rinsed
- handful of parsley, finely chopped
- handful of mint, finely chopped
- 100g (3½oz) cherry tomatoes, quartered
- grated zest and juice of 1 lemon
- 100g (scant ½ cup) Greek yogurt
- 1 tbsp tahini
- 1 tsp maple syrup
- pinch of chilli flakes
- salt and freshly ground black pepper

1 Preheat the air fryer to 200°C/400°F for 3 minutes.

2 Prick the sweet potatoes all over with a fork, then drizzle over 2 tablespoons olive oil and season with a little salt. Put the sweet potatoes into the air fryer basket and cook at 200°C/400°F for 30–35 minutes until softened.

3 Meanwhile, add the lentils, parsley, mint, tomatoes, lemon zest, and lemon juice to a bowl. Season with salt and freshly ground black pepper, then mix well and set aside.

4 To a small bowl, add the Greek yogurt, tahini, and maple syrup. Season with salt and freshly ground black pepper, mix well, and add a little water if it is looking too thick.

5 Cut the sweet potatoes open, then top with the yogurt and lentils. Sprinkle over a few chilli flakes and serve.

Swap it Swap the sweet potatoes for white potatoes, if you wish. Just add 20 minutes to the cooking time.

Sweet potatoes offer slow-release energy and beta-carotene, a pigment converted to vitamin A for skin, eye, and immune health.

Baked Feta

Kcals 390
Protein 25g
Fibre 17g
Saturated Fat 7g
Unsaturated Fat 5g

Serves 4

Prep + cook time:
15 minutes

- 2 x 400g (14oz) cans butter beans, drained and rinsed
- 2 x 400g (14oz) cans chopped tomatoes
- 1 red pepper, roughly chopped
- 1 tbsp dried oregano
- 200g (7oz) feta
- zest and juice of 1 lemon
- handful of basil
- salt and freshly ground black pepper

1 Preheat the air fryer to 180°C/350°F for 3 minutes.

2 In a dish that fits into the air fryer, add the butter beans, chopped tomatoes, red pepper, and oregano. Season with salt and freshly ground black pepper, then mix well and cook at 180°C/350°F for 4 minutes.

3 Place the feta on top and cook for a further 5 minutes until the feta is golden.

4 Squeeze over the lemon juice, top with the lemon zest and basil leaves, and serve.

Serve it This can be enjoyed with crusty bread or mixed into pasta, or simply served on its own.

Baking feta with tomatoes and beans creates a warming and nutrient-packed dish full of calcium, fibre, and flavour.

Chickpea Stew

Kcals 407
Protein 22g
Fibre 15g
Saturated Fat 2g
Unsaturated Fat 12g

Serves 4

Prep + cook time:
3 hours
10 minutes

- 1 tbsp extra virgin olive oil
- 1 onion, finely chopped
- 2 cloves of garlic, crushed
- 1 tsp smoked paprika
- ½ tsp cayenne pepper
- 2 x 400g (14oz) cans chickpeas
- 400g (14oz) can plum tomatoes
- 200ml (scant 1 cup) vegetable stock
- 2 tbsp sherry vinegar
- 200g (7oz) spinach
- 50g (generous ⅓ cup) toasted almonds
- salt and freshly ground black pepper

1 Add the olive oil to a large saucepan set over a low–medium heat. Once hot, add the onion and cook for 5 minutes until softened.

2 Add the garlic, paprika, and cayenne pepper, then cook for a further 1 minute until fragrant.

3 Tip the contents of the pan into the slow cooker. Add the chickpeas, along with the liquid from the cans, the plum tomatoes, vegetable stock, and sherry vinegar, then cook on high for 3 hours.

4 Season with salt and freshly ground black pepper, stir through the spinach until just wilted, then sprinkle over the toasted almonds and serve.

Keep it This will keep in the fridge for up to 4 days, and in the freezer for up to 3 months.

Chickpeas and spinach deliver fibre, iron, and plant protein in this comforting slow-cooker dish. Tomatoes and garlic add antioxidants and depth of flavour.

Lentil Ragù

Kcals 530
Protein 27g
Fibre 22g
Saturated Fat 1g
Unsaturated Fat 6g

Serves 4

Prep + cook time:
4 hours 30 minutes

- 40g (1½oz) dried porcini mushrooms
- 100ml (6½ tbsp) boiling water
- 1 tbsp extra virgin olive oil
- 1 onion, finely chopped
- 1 carrot, peeled and finely chopped
- 1 stick of celery, finely chopped
- 2 cloves of garlic, crushed
- 2 x 400g (14oz) cans green lentils, drained and rinsed
- 1 x 400g (14oz) can chopped tomatoes
- 1 sprig of rosemary
- 300g (10½oz) spaghetti
- salt and freshly ground black pepper

1 Put the porcini mushrooms into a measuring jug and pour the boiling water over the mushrooms. Set aside for 20 minutes.

2 Meanwhile, add the olive oil to a large frying pan set over a low–medium heat. Once hot, add the onion, carrot, celery, and garlic and cook for 10 minutes until the vegetables have softened.

3 Transfer the contents of the pan to the slow cooker. Add the green lentils, chopped tomatoes, rosemary, and porcini mushrooms, along with the soaking liquid. Cook on high for 4 hours, then season with salt and freshly ground black pepper.

4 When ready to serve, fill a large saucepan with water and bring to the boil. Once boiling, add the pasta and cook according to the packet instructions. Drain and serve with the ragù.

Keep it This ragù will keep well in the fridge for 4 days, or in the freezer for 3 months.

Lentils provide protein and fibre, while mushrooms and tomatoes add depth, richness, and antioxidants to this plant-based take on a family favourite.

AIR FRYER & SLOW COOKER

Chicken & Chorizo Casserole

Kcals 615
Protein 41g
Fibre 6.4g
Saturated Fat 11g
Unsaturated Fat 32g

Serves 4

Prep + cook time:
6 hours
20 minutes

- 1 tbsp extra virgin olive oil
- 1 onion, sliced
- 2 red peppers, sliced
- 4 cloves of garlic, crushed
- 1 tbsp smoked paprika
- 4 skinless, boneless chicken thighs
- 200g (7oz) cooking chorizo, cut into 1cm (½in) rounds
- 2 tbsp sun-dried tomato paste
- 100g (1 cup) pitted green olives
- 200ml (scant 1 cup) chicken stock
- 400g (14oz) can chopped tomatoes
- salt and freshly ground black pepper

1 Add the olive oil to a large frying pan set over a low–medium heat. Once hot, add the onion and peppers, then cook for 10 minutes until softened. Add the garlic and paprika, then cook for a further 1 minute until fragrant.

2 Tip the contents of the pan into the slow cooker. Add the chicken, chorizo, tomato paste, green olives, stock, and chopped tomatoes, then cook on low for 6 hours.

3 Season with salt and freshly ground black pepper, then serve.

Keep it This will freeze well for 3 months.

Chicken provides lean protein, while chorizo and olives offer bold flavours in this slow-cooked classic, which is packed with Mediterranean spice.

Minestrone

Kcals 549
Protein 26g
Fibre 12g
Saturated Fat 7g
Unsaturated Fat 13g

Serves 6

Prep + cook time:
3 hours 20 minutes

- 2 tbsp extra virgin olive oil
- 200g (7oz) pancetta, diced
- 2 carrots, finely chopped
- 2 celery sticks, finely chopped
- 1 onion, finely chopped
- 3 cloves of garlic, crushed
- 400g (14oz) can chopped tomatoes
- 1.5 litres (6 cups) vegetable or chicken stock
- 400g (14oz) can cannellini beans, drained and rinsed
- 400g (14oz) can kidney beans, drained and rinsed
- 2 bay leaves
- 1 sprig of rosemary
- 300g (10½oz) macaroni, or other small pasta
- 200g (7oz) spinach
- 3 tbsp finely grated Parmesan
- salt and freshly ground black pepper

1 Add the olive oil to a large frying pan set over a medium heat. Once hot, add the pancetta, then cook for 5 minutes until golden in colour. Add the carrot, celery, onion, and garlic, then cook for a further 5 minutes until slightly softened.

2 Tip the contents of the frying pan into the slow cooker. Add the chopped tomatoes, stock, cannellini beans, kidney beans, bay leaves, and rosemary sprig. Season with salt and freshly ground black pepper, and cook on high for 3 hours.

3 Add the pasta and cook for a further 7 minutes until al dente.

4 Stir through the spinach until just wilted, then sprinkle over the Parmesan and some freshly ground black pepper, and serve.

Keep it This will keep in the fridge for up to 4 days.

Packed with veg, beans, pasta, and herbs, this soup brings together fibre, plant diversity, and comfort in one tasty pot.

AIR FRYER & SLOW COOKER

Savoury Snacks

These Mediterranean snacks are great to have on hand to keep you going throughout the day, or even to enjoy as a starter before dinner. Why not try a selection of them next time you are making nibbles for a party?

Courgette Fries

Kcals 257
Protein 14g
Fibre 1.6g
Saturated Fat 3g
Unsaturated Fat 4g

Serves 4

Prep + cook time:
30 minutes

3 tbsp plain flour
2 eggs
150g (2 cups) dried breadcrumbs
2 courgettes, cut into 2cm (¾in) batons
3 tbsp finely grated Parmesan
1 tbsp dried oregano
olive oil spray
salt and freshly ground black pepper

1 Preheat the oven to 220°C (200°C fan/425°F/Gas 7).

2 Put the flour, eggs, and breadcrumbs into 3 separate shallow dishes. Season the flour with a pinch of salt and lightly beat the eggs with a fork.

3 Put a courgette baton in the flour and shake off the excess, then place into the egg, then into the breadcrumbs. Repeat this process with all of the courgette batons, lining them on a large baking tray as you go.

4 Spray liberally with the oil and put the tray into the oven, cooking for 20 minutes until golden in colour.

5 Remove from the oven, then sprinkle over the Parmesan and oregano. Season with salt and freshly ground black pepper, then serve.

Serve it These make for a delicious snack, or serve as part of an antipasti board.

Courgettes coated in breadcrumbs and Parmesan offer fibre and flavour with less fat than traditional fries. Great with a yogurt dip for extra protein.

Bruschetta

Kcals 384
Protein 10g
Fibre 3g
Saturated Fat 8g
Unsaturated Fat 21g

Serves 4

**Prep + cook time:
20 minutes**

1 ciabatta loaf, cut into thick slices
250g (9oz) tomatoes, chopped
1 tbsp balsamic vinegar
2 tbsp extra virgin olive oil
100g (3½oz) feta
handful of basil
salt and freshly ground black pepper

Pesto:

100g (3½oz) rocket
50ml (3½ tbsp) extra virgin olive oil
25g (3 tbsp) walnuts or pine nuts
10g (2½ tbsp) finely grated Parmesan, plus extra to serve
grated zest of 1 lemon and juice of ½ lemon
salt and freshly ground black pepper

1 Preheat the oven to 190°C (170°C fan/375°F/Gas 5).

2 Arrange the ciabatta slices on a baking tray and set aside.

3 Add the tomatoes to a baking dish, then drizzle over the balsamic vinegar and olive oil. Season with salt and freshly ground black pepper.

4 Cook the ciabatta and tomatoes in the oven for 10 minutes, then set aside.

5 Meanwhile, to a blender, add the rocket, olive oil, walnuts or pine nuts, Parmesan, lemon zest, and lemon juice. Season with salt and freshly ground black pepper, then blitz until combined.

6 Spread the pesto onto the ciabatta slices, then spoon over the tomatoes and crumble over the feta. Sprinkle over the basil, top with extra grated Parmesan and some freshly ground black pepper, and serve.

> Olive oil helps with the absorption of lycopene and antioxidants from tomatoes, while feta adds protein.

Dolmades

Kcals 224
Protein 16g
Fibre 3g
Saturated Fat 3g
Unsaturated Fat 3g

Serves 6

Prep + cook time:
1 hour

- 200g (generous 1 cup) long-grain rice
- 350g (¾lb) lamb mince
- 1 tbsp dried oregano
- 1 tsp ground cinnamon
- handful of parsley, roughly chopped
- 300g (10½oz) jarred vine leaves, drained and rinsed
- 2 lemons, thinly sliced into rounds
- 500ml (2 cups) chicken stock
- salt and freshly ground black pepper

1 To a bowl add the rice, lamb mince, oregano, cinnamon, and parsley. Season with salt and freshly ground black pepper, and mix well until combined.

2 Lay out the vine leaves on a flat surface. To the bottom half of a vine leaf, add a tablespoon of the filling. Start to roll the leaf up, then tuck in both sides, and continue to roll up until shaped like a cigar. Repeat until all the leaves and filling are used up.

3 Arrange the lemon slices on the bottom of a saucepan or flameproof casserole dish, then layer the dolmades on top. Pour over the chicken stock, then put a heatproof plate into the saucepan or casserole dish to ensure the dolmades are submerged in the chicken stock. Cover with a lid, bring to a gentle simmer, and cook for 30 minutes until tender and cooked through.

4 Serve with or without the chicken broth.

Serve it These make a tasty snack, or would be a great addition as part of a bigger spread.

Keep it These will keep in the fridge for up to 4 days.

Vine leaves stuffed with rice and lamb offer a satisfying mix of protein, iron, and fibre. Slow simmering with herbs and lemon keeps this dish light yet full of flavour.

SAVOURY SNACKS

Kale Crisps

Kcals	81
Protein	2g
Fibre	2.5g
Saturated Fat	1g
Unsaturated Fat	6g

Serves 4

Prep + cook time:
15 minutes

200g (7oz) kale, stalks removed, roughly chopped
2 tbsp extra virgin olive oil
1 tbsp paprika
1 tsp ground cumin
1 tsp sesame seeds
salt

1 Preheat the oven to 200°C (180°C fan/400°F/Gas 6).

2 Spread the kale out on a large baking tray, drizzle over the olive oil, and scrunch the kale with your hands.

3 Sprinkle over the paprika, cumin, and sesame seeds. Cook in the oven for 10 minutes until crispy, then serve.

Keep it These will keep in an airtight container for 3 days.

> Kale is a great source of vitamin K and fibre. Roasting it with olive oil keeps the flavour high and the prep low, a smart swap for traditional crisps.

SAVOURY SNACKS

Pitta Nachos

Kcals 515
Protein 47g
Fibre 6g
Saturated Fat 5g
Unsaturated Fat 12g

Serves 4

Prep + cook time: 20 minutes

- 4 pitta breads, cut into triangles
- 3 tbsp extra virgin olive oil
- 500g (1lb 2oz) beef mince
- 1 clove of garlic, crushed
- 1 tbsp ground cumin
- 1 tbsp harissa
- ½ cucumber, finely diced
- ½ red onion, finely diced
- 1 large tomato, finely chopped
- handful of parsley, finely chopped
- 2 tbsp pomegranate seeds
- juice of 1 lemon
- salt and freshly ground black pepper

1 Preheat the oven to 200°C (180°C fan/400°F/Gas 6).

2 Arrange the pitta bread triangles on a large baking tray in a single layer, if possible. Drizzle over 2 tablespoons olive oil, then put into the oven. Cook for 10 minutes until golden and crispy. Remove and set aside to cool.

3 Meanwhile, add the remaining 1 tablespoon olive oil to a frying pan set over a medium-high heat. Add the beef mince, then cook for 5 minutes until browned. Add in the garlic, cumin, and harissa. Season with salt and freshly ground black pepper and cook for a further 2 minutes, or until the mince is cooked through. Remove from the heat and set aside.

4 Meanwhile, add the cucumber, red onion, tomato, parsley, pomegranate seeds, and lemon juice to a bowl. Season with salt and freshly ground black pepper, mix well, and set aside.

5 Load the pitta chips onto a platter, top with the beef mince and salad, then serve.

Serve it These would go really well with the tzatziki on page 148.

> Toasted pitta makes a lighter alternative to crisps, while spiced mince adds protein and iron. Fresh Med-inspired toppings – like tomato, parsley, and pomegranate – boost plant variety and flavour.

SAVOURY SNACKS

Grissini

Kcals	391
Protein	11g
Fibre	3g
Saturated Fat	4g
Unsaturated Fat	11g

Serves 6

Prep + cook time:
30 minutes, plus proving time

- 400g (scant 3 cups) strong white bread flour, plus extra for dusting
- 80ml (⅓ cup) extra virgin olive oil
- 1 tsp fennel seeds
- 7g (¼oz) instant dried yeast
- 50g (¾ cup) finely grated Parmesan
- 1 tbsp honey
- 1 tsp salt

1 Put the flour, olive oil, fennel seeds, dried yeast, Parmesan, honey, and salt into a bowl. Add 140ml (½ cup plus 1 tbsp) lukewarm water, then mix well and knead until you have a smooth ball. Cover with a tea towel, and leave for around an hour until doubled in size.

2 Preheat the oven to 200°C (180°C fan/400°F/Gas 6) and line a large baking tray with baking parchment.

3 Dust the work surface with a little flour, then roll out the dough into a rectangle about 1cm (½in) thick. Cut into long strips that are about 2cm (¾in) wide. Carefully put onto the lined baking tray and bake for 15 minutes until golden. Leave to cool, then serve.

Keep it These will keep in an airtight container for 4 days.

These homemade breadsticks offer a crisp, satisfying crunch with the added bonus of olive oil and Parmesan. Ideal for pairing with dips or cheese for a snack with substance.

Courgettes with Red Pepper Dip

Kcals 261
Protein 4g
Fibre 2g
Saturated Fat 3g
Unsaturated Fat 18g

Serves 4

Prep + cook time:
15 minutes

- 40g (scant ⅓ cup) blanched almonds
- 65ml (4½ tbsp) extra virgin olive oil, plus extra to serve
- 2 courgettes, thinly sliced
- 170g (6oz) jarred roasted red peppers
- ½ clove of garlic
- 1 tsp smoked paprika
- 1 tbsp sherry vinegar
- salt and freshly ground black pepper

To serve (optional):
crostini or nachos
pickles

1 Preheat the oven to 200°C (180°C fan/400°F/Gas 6).

2 Put the almonds onto a small baking dish, then cook in the oven for 5 minutes until golden in colour. Set aside.

3 Add 1 tablespoon olive oil to a frying pan set over a medium heat. Once hot, add the courgettes and cook for 5 minutes until softened, then set aside.

4 Add three-quarters of the almonds to a blender with the jarred peppers, garlic, paprika, sherry vinegar, and remaining 50ml (3½ tbsp) olive oil. Season with salt and freshly ground black pepper. Pulse until combined, but not totally smooth.

5 Roughly chop the remaining almonds and set aside.

6 Spread the red pepper dip over a small serving platter, then top with the courgettes. Sprinkle over the remaining chopped almonds and drizzle over a little more olive oil. Serve with crostini or nachos for dipping and some pickles, if liked.

Serve it This dip would also make a delicious side dish to some white fish.

Courgettes are light, hydrating, and rich in vitamin C and potassium. Served with a roasted red pepper and tahini dip, there's a dose of fibre in every bite.

Tzatziki

Kcals 112
Protein 10g
Fibre 1g
Saturated Fat 6g
Unsaturated Fat 4g

Serves 4

Prep time:
5 minutes

½ cucumber
200g (scant 1 cup) Greek yogurt
1 clove of garlic, crushed
grated zest of 1 lemon
handful of mint, finely chopped
salt and freshly ground black pepper

To serve (optional):
olive oil
crackers or taralli

1 Grate the cucumber, then squeeze out the water with your hands.

2 Add most of the grated cucumber to a bowl (reserving a little for serving). Add the Greek yogurt, garlic, most of the lemon zest (reserving a pinch for serving), and mint. Season with salt and freshly ground black pepper and stir together.

3 Top with the reserved grated cucumber, reserved lemon zest, a pinch of freshly ground black pepper, and a drizzle of olive oil, and serve with crackers or taralli, if liked.

Serve it This is a versatile dip and goes well with most proteins. Try it with the stifado on page 100.

Keep it This will keep in the fridge for up to 3 days.

This traditional dip is made with strained yogurt, offering more protein and calcium than many creamy dips. Cucumber, garlic, and mint add freshness and flavour. It's a light, nourishing staple of Mediterranean food culture.

Desserts

In this dessert selection you will find a selection of sweet treats that are delicious yet still nourishing. From a refreshing Watermelon Granita and Greek Yogurt Bark to a delicious Orange Olive Oil Cake and crunchy Biscotti, these are the perfect treats to satisfy any sweet cravings!

Orange Olive Oil Cake

Kcals 348
Protein 4.1g
Fibre 0.7g
Saturated Fat 3g
Unsaturated Fat 15g

Serves 8

Prep + cook time:
1 hour

- 200g (1 cup) caster sugar
- grated zest and juice of 1 orange
- 140ml (scant ⅔ cup) extra virgin olive oil, plus extra for lining
- 2 large eggs
- 1 tsp vanilla extract
- 100g (scant ½ cup) natural yogurt
- 100g (generous ¾ cup) plain flour
- 1 tsp baking powder

Topping:
- 50g (scant ½ cup) icing sugar
- juice of 1 orange
- edible flowers (optional)

1 Preheat the oven to 180°C (160°C fan/350°F/Gas 4).

2 Line a 900g (2lb) loaf tin with baking parchment and set aside.

3 To a large bowl (or stand mixer fitted with the whisk attachment) add the sugar, orange zest, orange juice, olive oil, eggs, vanilla extract, and yogurt. Whisk for 1 minute until combined.

4 Sift the flour and baking powder into the bowl, and fold in with a spatula until well combined.

5 Transfer the mixture to the tin, and bake for 45 minutes until a skewer comes out clean when inserted.

6 Leave to cool slightly in the tin, before turning out onto a wire rack to cool completely.

7 Meanwhile, to a small bowl, add the icing sugar and orange juice, then mix well until you have a thick but runny icing. Pour this over the cake, and top with edible flowers, if liked.

Swap it This would also work well with grapefruit, or try using blood oranges when in season.

Olive oil provides unsaturated fats, while yogurt adds protein and calcium here. The citrus zest brings brightness, to this light dessert.

Honey Cake

Kcals	516
Protein	5g
Fibre	1g
Saturated Fat	17g
Unsaturated Fat	17g

Serves 12

Prep + cook time:
1 hour, plus cooling time

200g (1¾ sticks) unsalted butter
150g (¾ cup) light soft brown sugar
200g (⅔ cup) honey, plus extra to drizzle
100ml (6½ tbsp) vegetable oil, plus extra for greasing
2 large eggs
350g (2¾ cups) plain flour
2 tsp baking powder
½ tsp flaky salt

Topping:

200g (scant 1 cup) crème fraîche
100ml (6½ tbsp) double cream
2 tsp vanilla extract
3 tbsp thyme leaves
2 tbsp walnut halves

The natural sweetness of honey complements the Mediterranean flavours of thyme, olive oil, and crème fraîche.

1 Preheat the oven to 180°C (160°C fan/350°F/Gas 4). Grease and line a 20cm (8in) round cake tin with baking parchment.

2 To a saucepan, add the butter, sugar, and honey. Set over a low heat and cook for 4 minutes until the sugar has dissolved, then increase the heat to medium and cook for a further 3 minutes until the mixture has slightly darkened in colour. Remove from the heat and set aside to cool for 5 minutes.

3 To a bowl, add the vegetable oil and eggs. Pour over the honey mixture, then whisk well until smooth. Sift the flour over, then add the baking powder and salt. Fold the mix well with a spatula until you can no longer see any of the white flour.

4 Transfer the mix to the cake tin and bake, on the middle shelf of the oven, for 40 minutes until a skewer comes out clean when inserted. Leave to cool for 20 minutes, then transfer to a wire rack to cool completely.

5 Meanwhile, for the topping, add the crème fraîche, double cream, and vanilla to a bowl. Whisk well until thick.

6 Spread the topping over the top of the cooled cake, drizzle over a little more honey, and add the thyme and walnuts.

Keep it This will keep in the fridge for up to 4 days.

Baklava Bites

Kcals	453
Protein	6g
Fibre	2g
Saturated Fat	8g
Unsaturated Fat	20g

Makes 8

Prep + cook time:
1 hour

90g (6½ tbsp) unsalted butter
2 tbsp light soft brown sugar
1 tsp ground cinnamon
100g (¾ cup) pistachios, finely blitzed
100g (¾ cup) walnut halves, finely blitzed
4 sheets filo pastry
2 tbsp vegetable oil

Syrup:
200g (1 cup) caster sugar
20g (generous 1 tbsp) honey

1 Preheat the oven to 180°C (160°C fan/350°F/Gas 4).

2 In a small saucepan, melt the butter, sugar, and cinnamon, over a gentle heat. Add the pistachios and walnuts, then mix through and set aside to cool.

3 Lay one piece of filo pastry on the work surface, then brush it with vegetable oil. Layer another piece of pastry on top, and brush with more vegetable oil. Repeat this with all 4 sheets of filo.

4 With one of the long sides of layered pastry facing you, cut the stack vertically into 4 strips.

5 Divide the nut mixture equally among the 4 filo strips, placing the mixture at the bottom of each strip. Fold the sides of the pastry inwards, then roll upwards from the bottom until you reach the top, so all the filling in enclosed. Repeat with all 4 pastries, then put into a baking dish. Brush the pastry with a little more oil and set aside.

6 To a small saucepan, add the caster sugar, honey, and 200ml (scant 1 cup) water, then set over a low heat to dissolve the sugar. Once dissolved, increase the heat and let it bubble away for about 20 minutes until syrupy.

7 Meanwhile, put the baklava into the oven and cook for 30–35 minutes until golden. Remove the baklava from the oven and pour over the syrup. Leave to cool, then cut each piece in half to serve.

Nuts provide protein, fibre, and heart-healthy fats in this tasty dessert that captures the rich flavours of traditional Mediterranean baking.

DESSERTS

Pear Galette

Kcals	303
Prote	4.7g
Fibre	3.6g
Saturated Fat	6g
Unsaturated Fat	6g

Serves 6

Prep + cook time:
30 minutes

- 4 pears, cored and sliced
- 1 tsp vanilla extract
- 3 tbsp golden caster sugar
- 1 tbsp cornflour
- 1 tsp ground cinnamon
- 320g (11oz) puff pastry sheet
- 1 egg
- 1 tbsp honey

To serve (optional):
crème fraîche or ice cream

1 Preheat the oven to 200°C (180°C fan/400°F/Gas 6).

2 To a bowl, add the pear slices, vanilla extract, sugar, cornflour, and cinnamon, then mix well and set aside.

3 Unroll the pastry sheet and place onto a large baking tray. Cut the biggest circle you can from the sheet, then put the filling into the centre of the circle, leaving a 6cm (2½in) border. Fold the edges of the pastry into the centre, overlapping the filling.

4 Crack the egg into a small bowl and whisk well, then brush the pastry border with the egg wash.

5 Put into the oven and cook for 20 minutes until the pastry is golden.

6 Drizzle over the honey, and serve with crème fraîche or ice cream, if you like.

Swap it Plums or apricots would also work here.

Pears provide soluble fibre like pectin, which supports gut health and blood-sugar balance. Paired with a crisp pastry, this dessert offers sweetness without feeling too heavy.

Peach Melba

Kcals 480
Protein 5.4g
Fibre 8g
Saturated Fat 0g
Unsaturated Fat 8g

Serves 4

Prep + cook time:
15 minutes

300g (1½ cups) caster sugar
1 tbsp vanilla extract
juice of ½ lemon
4 peaches, halved
500g (1lb 2oz) raspberries
50g (⅔ cup) flaked toasted almonds

To serve (optional):
vanilla ice cream

1 To a large saucepan add 600ml (2½ cups) water along with the caster sugar, vanilla extract, and lemon juice. Bring the water to a steady simmer until you see the sugar dissolve, then bring to the boil for a few minutes until syrupy. Reduce the heat again to a steady simmer.

2 Add the peaches to the syrup and cook for 5 minutes. Remove with a slotted spoon and leave until cool enough to handle. Remove the skins from the peaches and set aside.

3 Add the raspberries to a blender, add in a ladle of the syrup, and blitz until smooth. Set aside.

4 Serve the peaches with the raspberry coulis and top with flaked almonds. Serve with ice cream, if you like.

Swap it Plums would also work well here.

Poached peaches, raspberries, and flaked almonds – this light, summery dish is naturally full of fibre and vitamin C. This is a sweet option that still feels nourishing.

Watermelon Granita

Kcals 142
Protein 1.2g
Fibre 1.1g
Saturated Fat 0g
Unsaturated Fat 1g

Serves 4

Prep time: 5 minutes, plus freezing time

1 small watermelon
50g (¼ cup) caster sugar
grated zest and juice of 2 limes

1 Cut off the watermelon rind, then cut the watermelon flesh into chunks.

2 Add to a blender with the sugar, lime zest, and lime juice. Blitz until smooth, then pour into a small freezer-proof container.

3 Put into the freezer for 1 hour, then remove and scrape with a fork. Repeat this process once more, then serve once frozen.

Keep it This will keep in the freezer for up to 3 months.

Watermelon is hydrating and naturally rich in antioxidants like lycopene. This granita is a refreshing way to cool down with no fuss and no added sugar.

Almond & Pistachio Biscotti

Kcals 480
Protein 14g
Fibre 4g
Saturated Fat 3g
Unsaturated Fat 14g

Serves 4

Prep + cook time:
1 hour

- 200g (1½ cups) plain flour
- 80g (6½ tbsp) soft brown sugar
- ½ tsp baking powder
- 80g (generous ½ cup) pistachios
- 20 blanched almonds
- grated zest of 1 orange
- 1 tsp ground cinnamon
- ½ tsp salt
- 2 tbsp honey
- 2 eggs

1 Preheat the oven to 180°C (160°C fan/350°F/Gas 4) and line a large baking tray with baking parchment.

2 To a bowl, add the flour, sugar, baking powder, pistachios, almonds, irange zest, cinnamon, and salt. Make a well in the middle, then add the honey and eggs. Mix well with your hands to bring the dough together, then divide the dough into 2 balls.

3 Roll each of the balls into a log shape, measuring about 20cm (8in) in length. Place both of the logs onto the lined baking tray, making sure they are spaced out.

4 Bake in the oven for 20 minutes, then remove from the oven, then turn the temperature down to 120°C (100°C fan/250°F/Gas ½).

5 Cut the logs diagonally into slices. Flip the slices over so they are cut-side up, then put back into the oven to bake for a further 20 minutes. Leave to cool, then serve.

Keep it These will keep in an airtight container for 1 week.

These are made with nuts rich in vitamin E and polyphenols, supporting heart and skin health. Orange zest and cinnamon add a flavourful edge without excess sugar.

Chocolate-covered Dates

Kcals 344
Protein 6g
Fibre 5g
Saturated Fat 9g
Unsaturated Fat 10g

Serves 6

Prep + cook time:
20 minutes, plus chilling time

200g (7oz) dark chocolate
200g (7oz) pitted dates
50g (generous ⅓ cup) pistachios, roughly chopped

1 Melt the chocolate in a heatproof bowl set over a saucepan of gently simmering water, making sure the bottom of the bowl doesn't touch the water.

2 Dip the dates into the melted chocolate, put onto a baking tray, then sprinkle over the chopped pistachios.

3 Leave in the fridge for at least an hour until set.

Keep it These will keep in the fridge for up to 5 days, or in the freezer for up to 3 months.

> Dates provide natural sweetness, fibre, and potassium, while dark chocolate and pistachios offer polyphenols and healthy fats.

DESSERTS

Greek Yogurt Bark

Kcals 163
Protein 11g
Fibre 2g
Saturated Fat 1g
Unsaturated Fat 4g

Serves 6

Prep time: 10 minutes, plus setting time

500g (2¼ cups) Greek yogurt
100g (3½oz) raspberries
100g (3½oz) blueberries
100g (3½oz) pitted dates, halved
50g (generous ⅓ cup) pistachios or walnut halves, roughly chopped

1 Line a large baking tray with baking parchment, then spread the Greek yogurt over the parchment.

2 Top with the raspberries, blueberries, dates, and nuts. Put the tray into the freezer for at least 1 hour until set.

3 Cut into shards and serve.

Keep it This will keep in the freezer for up to 3 months.

Fresh berries add colour and antioxidants to this refreshing, nutrient-dense sweet treat, which is also full of calcium and protein thanks to the Greek yogurt.

Conversion Charts

MEASURES

North America, New Zealand, and the United Kingdom use a 5ml teaspoon and a 15ml tablespoon. North American measuring cups hold approximately 240ml. An Australian metric measuring cup holds approximately 250ml; one Australian metric tablespoon holds 20ml; one Australian metric teaspoon holds 5ml.

The difference between one country's measuring cups and another's is within a two- or three-teaspoon variance and will not affect your cooking results. All cup and spoon measurements are level.

The most accurate way of measuring dry ingredients is to weigh them.

When measuring liquids, use a clear glass or plastic jug with metric markings. We use extra-large eggs with an average weight of 60g each.

DRY MEASURES

metric	imperial
15g	½oz
30g	1oz
60g	2oz
90g	3oz
125g	4oz (¼lb)
155g	5oz
185g	6oz
220g	7oz
250g	8oz (½lb)
280g	9oz
315g	10oz
345g	11oz
375g	12oz (¾lb)
410g	13oz
440g	14oz
470g	15oz
500g	16oz (1lb)
750g	24oz (1½lb)
1kg	32oz (2lb)

LIQUID MEASURES

metric	imperial
30ml	1 fluid oz
60ml	2 fluid oz
100ml	3 fluid oz
125ml	4 fluid oz
150ml	5 fluid oz
190ml	6 fluid oz
250ml	8 fluid oz
300ml	10 fluid oz
500ml	16 fluid oz
600ml	20 fluid oz
1000ml (1 litre)	1¾ pints

LENGTH MEASURES

metric	imperial
3mm	⅛in
6mm	¼in
1cm	½in
2cm	¾in
2.5cm	1in
5cm	2in
6cm	2½in
8cm	3in
10cm	4in
13cm	5in
15cm	6in
18cm	7in
20cm	8in
22cm	9in
25cm	10in
28cm	11in
30cm	12in (1ft)

Index

A
air fryer recipes 115–31
almond
  almond & pistachio biscotti 164, **165**
  chickpea stew 124, **125**
  courgettes with red pepper dip **146**, 147
  peach melba **160**, 161
anchovy, pissaladière 68, **69**
anti-inflammatory foods 7
aubergine
  aubergine parmigiana 102, **103**
  caponata pasta **64**, 65
  cauliflower salad bowl **46**, 47
  ratatouille 112, **113**

B
baklava bites **156**, 157
basil 28, 32, 38, 48, 53, 62, 78, 102, 109, 125, 138
batch cooking 91–112
bean(s)
  baked feta **122**, 123
  gigantes plaki **36**, 37
  lemony borlotti bean broth 58, **59**
  minestrone **130**, 131
  see also green bean
beef
  harissa beef meatballs 84, **85**
  pitta nachos **142**, 143
  stifado 100, **101**
biscotti, almond & pistachio 164, **165**
blood-sugar control 7, 10
"blue zones" 7
blueberry
  French toast 20, **21**
  Greek yogurt bark 168, **169**
borlotti bean lemony broth 58, **59**
bread sticks 144, **145**
breadcrumbs
  aubergine parmigiana 102, **103**
  chicken meatballs **108**, 109
  courgette fries 134, **135**
  harissa beef meatballs 84, **85**

spinach fritters with courgette yogurt **96**, 97
breakfast 17–32
broth, lemony borlotti bean 58, **59**
bruschetta 136, **137**
bulgur wheat
  harissa salmon 74, **75**
  slow-cooked lamb shoulder **104**, 105
  spinach fritters **96**, 97
  tabbouleh salad 56, **57**
butter, garlic **50**, 51
butter bean
  baked feta **122**, 123
  gigantes plaki **36**, 37
butternut squash tagine **72**, 73

C
cabbage, chicken gyros **116**, 117
cakes
  honey cake 154, **155**
  orange olive oil cake **152**, 153
capers
  caponata pasta **64**, 65
  lemon & garlic chicken traybake **66**, 67
  Marbella chicken 78, **79**
  steamed sea bass with potatoes **76**, 77
  tuna niçoise salad **42**, 43
  watermelon & halloumi salad 38, **39**
caponata pasta **64**, 65
carrot
  lentil ragù **126**, 127
  minestrone **130**, 131
casserole, chicken & chorizo **128**, 129
cauliflower salad bowl **46**, 47
celery
  gigantes plaki **36**, 37
  lentil ragù **126**, 127
  minestrone **130**, 131
cheese
  aubergine parmigiana 102, **103**
  cheesy polenta with mushrooms **82**, 83

figs with ricotta on toast **18**, 19
flatbread pizza 48, **49**
spinach lasagne **106**, 107
see also feta cheese; halloumi; Parmesan cheese
chicken
  chicken & chorizo casserole **128**, 129
  chicken gyros **116**, 117
  chicken meatballs **108**, 109
  lemon & garlic chicken traybake **66**, 67
  Marbella chicken 78, **79**
chickpea flour, farinata 28, **29**
chickpea(s)
  chickpea & halloumi salad **118**, 119
  chickpea stew 124, **125**
  falafels 92, **93**
  spiced butternut squash tagine **72**, 73
chives
  green salad **40**, 41
  lemony borlotti bean broth 58, **59**
  pan con tomate 24, **25**
  steamed sea bass with potatoes **76**, 77
chocolate-covered dates 166, **167**
chorizo & chicken casserole **128**, 129
cinnamon
  almond & pistachio biscotti 164, **165**
  baklava bites **156**, 157
  French toast 20, **21**
clam(s)
  seafood paella **86**, 87
  spaghetti vongole **88**, 89
cod
  seafood paella **86**, 87
  Spanish-style fish stew 54, **55**
coriander (fresh)
  butternut squash tagine **72**, 73
  harissa salmon 74, **75**
courgette
  caponata pasta **64**, 65
  cauliflower salad bowl **46**, 47

chickpea & halloumi salad **118**, 119
courgette fries 134, **135**
courgette yogurt **96**, 97
courgettes with red pepper dip **146**, 147
frittata 32, **33**
lemony borlotti bean broth 58, **59**
ratatouille 112, **113**
roasted potato salad **52**, 53
spiced butternut squash tagine **72**, 73
couscous stuffed peppers 62, **63**
crème fraîche, honey cake 154, **155**
crisps, kale 140, **141**
cucumber
  Greek salad 94, **95**
  pitta nachos **142**, 143
  turkey kebabs 80, **81**
  tzatziki 148, **149**
  watermelon & halloumi salad 38, **39**

D

date(s)
  chocolate-covered dates 166, **167**
  Greek yogurt bark 168, **169**
desserts 151–68
dill 31, 38, 41, 43, 53, 58, 62, 97, 111
dinners, midweek 61–89
dip, red pepper **146**, 147
dolmades **140**, 141

E

egg
  almond & pistachio biscotti 164, **165**
  frittata 32, **33**
  greens filo pie **110**, 111
  harissa beef meatballs 84, **85**
  honey cake 154, **155**
  orange olive oil cake **152**, 153
  pear galette 158, **159**
  pissaladière 68, **69**
  spanakopita egg muffins **22**, 23

Spanish tortilla **40**, 41
spinach fritters with courgette yogurt **96**, 97
spring green shakshuka **26**, 27
Turkish eggs **30**, 31
equipment 14

F

falafels 92, **93**
farinata 28, **29**
fats, dietary 8, 10
feta cheese
  baked feta **122**, 123
  bruschetta 136, **137**
  Greek salad 94, **95**
  greens filo pie **110**, 111
  herby couscous stuffed peppers 62, **63**
  spanakopita egg muffins **22**, 23
  spinach fritters with courgette yogurt **96**, 97
  spring green shakshuka **26**, 27
fibre 10
fig(s) with ricotta on toast **18**, 19
filo pastry
  baklava bites **156**, 157
  greens filo pie **110**, 111
fish
  harissa salmon 74, **75**
  seafood paella **86**, 87
  Spanish-style fish stew 54, **55**
  steamed sea bass with potatoes **76**, 77
  tuna niçoise salad **42**, 43
flatbread
  chicken gyros **116**, 117
  flatbread pizza 48, **49**
  turkey kebabs 80, **81**
focaccia 98, **99**
French toast 20, **21**
fries, courgette 134, **135**
frittata 32, **33**
fritters, spinach **96**, 97

G

galette, pear 158, **159**
garlic
  crispy shallots and garlic **30**, 31
  garlic butter prawns **50**, 51

lemon & garlic chicken traybake **66**, 67
pesto 48, **49**
gigantes plaki **36**, 37
grain(s)
  chickpea & halloumi salad **118**, 119
  harissa beef meatballs 84, **85**
granita, watermelon 162, **163**
Greek salad 94, **95**
Greek yogurt
  baked sweet potatoes **120**, 121
  cauliflower salad bowl **46**, 47
  chicken gyros **116**, 117
  courgette yogurt **96**, 97
  Greek yogurt bark 168, **169**
  Turkish eggs **30**, 31
  tzatziki 148, **149**
green bean
  harissa salmon 74, **75**
  lemon & garlic chicken traybake **66**, 67
  tuna niçoise salad **42**, 43
greens
  greens filo pie **110**, 111
  spring green shakshuka **26**, 27
grissini 144, **145**
gyros, chicken **116**, 117

H

halloumi
  chickpea & halloumi salad **118**, 119
  halloumi wraps 44, **45**
  watermelon & halloumi salad 38, **39**
ham *see* Parma ham
harissa
  harissa beef meatballs 84, **85**
  harissa salmon 74, **75**
  pitta nachos **142**, 143
  spiced butternut squash tagine **72**, 73
herby couscous stuffed peppers 62, **63**
honey
  almond & pistachio biscotti 164, **165**
  figs with ricotta on toast **18**, 19
  honey cake 154, **155**

lemon & garlic chicken traybake **66**, 67
pear galette 158, **159**
syrups **156**, 157
watermelon & halloumi salad 38, **39**

I
icing **152**, 153

K
kale crisps 140, **141**
kebabs, turkey 80, **81**

L
lamb
  dolmades **138**, 139
  slow-cooked lamb shoulder **104**, 105
larders 14
lasagne, spinach **106**, 107
lemon
  dolmades **138**, 139
  lemon & garlic chicken traybake **66**, 67
  lemony borlotti bean broth 58, **59**
lentil(s)
  baked sweet potatoes **120**, 121
  lentil ragù **126**, 127
lettuce
  halloumi wraps 44, **45**
  turkey kebabs 80, **81**
lunches 35–59

M
Marbella chicken 78, **79**
mayo, mustard **76**, 77
meal planner 12–13
meal prep recipes 91–112
meatballs
  chicken meatballs **108**, 109
  harissa beef meatballs 84, **85**
Mediterranean diet 7, 8, 9
minestrone **130**, 131
mint 44, 56, 62, 109, 123, 148

mozzarella cheese
  aubergine parmigiana 102, **103**
  flatbread pizza 48, **49**
  spinach lasagne **106**, 107
muffins, spanakopita egg **22**, 23
mushroom
  cheesy polenta with mushrooms **82**, 83
  lentil ragù **126**, 127
  mushroom risotto **70**, 71
mussels
  seafood paella **86**, 87
  Spanish-style fish stew 54, **55**
mustard mayo **76**, 77

N
nachos, pitta **142**, 143
niçoise salad, tuna **42**, 43
nutrition 10

O
olive oil cake, orange **152**, 153
olive(s)
  caponata pasta **64**, 65
  chicken & chorizo casserole **128**, 129
  flatbread pizza 48, **49**
  Greek salad 94, **95**
  herby couscous stuffed peppers 62, **63**
  lemon & garlic chicken traybake **66**, 67
  Marbella chicken 78, **79**
  pissaladière 68, **69**
  roasted potato salad **52**, 53
  spiced butternut squash tagine **72**, 73
  steamed sea bass with potatoes **76**, 77
  tuna niçoise salad **42**, 43
orange
  almond & pistachio biscotti 164, **165**
  orange olive oil cake **152**, 153

P
paella, seafood **86**, 87
pan con tomate 24, **25**

pancetta, minestrone **130**, 131
Parma ham, flatbread pizza 48, **49**
Parmesan cheese
  aubergine parmigiana 102, **103**
  caponata pasta **64**, 65
  cheesy polenta with mushrooms **82**, 83
  courgette fries 134, **135**
  frittata 32, **33**
  greens filo pie **110**, 111
  grissini 146, **147**
  minestrone **130**, 131
  mushroom risotto **70**, 71
  pesto 48, **49**, 136, **137**
  spinach lasagne **106**, 107
parmigiana, aubergine 102, **103**
parsley
  baked sweet potatoes **122**, 123
  butternut squash tagine **72**, 73
  cheesy polenta with mushrooms **82**, 83
  chicken meatballs **108**, 109
  dolmades **138**, 139
  falafels 92, **93**
  farinata 28, **29**
  frittata 32, **33**
  garlic butter prawns **50**, 51
  gigantes plaki **36**, 37
  greens filo pie **110**, 111
  harissa beef meatballs 84, **85**
  herby couscous stuffed peppers 62, **63**
  lemon & garlic chicken traybake **66**, 67
  mushroom risotto **70**, 71
  pitta nachos **142**, 143
  seafood paella **86**, 87
  spaghetti vongole **88**, 89
  spanakopita egg muffins **22**, 23
  Spanish-style fish stew 54, **55**
  spring green shakshuka **26**, 27
  stifado 100, **101**
  tabbouleh salad 56, **57**
  turkey kebabs 80, **81**
passata
  flatbread pizza 48, **49**
  stifado 100, **101**
pasta
  caponata pasta **64**, 65
  lentil ragù **126**, 127

minestrone **130**, 131
spaghetti vongole **88**, 89
spinach lasagne **106**, 107
pastry *see* filo pastry; puff pastry
peach melba **160**, 161
pear galette 158, **159**
pepper (bell)
  baked feta **122**, 123
  chicken & chorizo casserole **128**, 129
  chickpea & halloumi salad **118**, 119
  Greek salad 94, **95**
  herby couscous stuffed peppers 62, **63**
  red pepper dip **146**, 147
  roasted potato salad **52**, 53
  seafood paella **86**, 87
pesto 48, **49**, 136, **137**
  spinach lasagne **106**, 107
pie, greens filo **110**, 111
pine nuts
  caponata pasta **64**, 65
  pesto 48, **49**, 136, **137**
pissaladière 68, **69**
pistachio
  almond & pistachio biscotti 164, **165**
  baklava bites **156**, 157
  chocolate-covered dates 166, **167**
  Greek yogurt bark 168, **169**
pitta nachos **142**, 143
pizza, flatbread 48, **49**
polenta, cheesy polenta with mushrooms **82**, 83
pomegranate seeds
  halloumi wraps 44, **45**
  pitta nachos **142**, 143
pork, harissa beef meatballs 84, **85**
potato
  lemon & garlic chicken traybake **66**, 67
  roasted potato salad **52**, 53
  Spanish tortilla **40**, 41
  steamed sea bass with potatoes **76**, 77
  tuna niçoise salad **42**, 43
prawn
  garlic butter prawns **50**, 51
  seafood paella **86**, 87
  Spanish-style fish stew 54, **55**
puff pastry
  pear galette 158, **159**
  pissaladière 68, **69**

Q

quinoa
  cauliflower salad bowl **46**, 47
  spinach fritters with courgette yogurt **96**, 97
  watermelon & halloumi salad 38, **39**

R

ragù, lentil **126**, 127
raspberry
  French toast 20, **21**
  Greek yogurt bark 168, **169**
  peach melba **160**, 161
ratatouille 112, **113**
red cabbage, chicken gyros **116**, 117
rice
  dolmades **138**, 139
  mushroom risotto **70**, 71
  seafood paella **86**, 87
ricotta, figs with ricotta on toast **18**, 19
risotto, mushroom **70**, 71
rocket
  chickpea & halloumi salad **118**, 119
  green salad **40**, 41
  pesto 138, **139**

S

salads
  cauliflower salad bowl **46**, 47
  chickpea & halloumi salad **118**, 119
  Greek salad 94, **95**
  green salad **40**, 41
  roasted potato salad **52**, 53
  tabbouleh salad 56, **57**
  tuna niçoise salad **42**, 43
  watermelon & halloumi salad 38, **39**

salmon, harissa 74, **75**
sea bass, steamed sea bass with potatoes **76**, 77
seafood paella **86**, 87
shakshuka, spring green **26**, 27
shallot(s), crispy shallots and garlic **30**, 31
slow cooker recipes 115–31
snacks, savoury 133–48
soup, minestrone **130**, 131
spaghetti vongole **88**, 89
spanakopita egg muffins **22**, 23
Spanish-style fish stew 54, **55**
Spanish tortilla **40**, 41
spinach
  chickpea stew 124, **125**
  green salad **40**, 41
  greens filo pie **110**, 111
  lemony borlotti bean broth 58, **59**
  minestrone **130**, 131
  spanakopita egg muffins **22**, 23
  spinach fritters with courgette yogurt **96**, 97
  spinach lasagne **106**, 107
  spring green shakshuka **26**, 27
spring green shakshuka **26**, 27
stew
  chickpea stew 124, **125**
  Spanish-style fish stew 54, **55**
stifado 100, **101**
sweet potato, baked **120**, 121
syrups **156**, 157

T

tabbouleh salad 56, **57**
tagine, butternut squash **72**, 73
tahini
  baked sweet potatoes **120**, 121
  cauliflower salad bowl **46**, 47
thyme
  honey cake 154, **155**
  pear galette 158, **159**
toast
  figs with ricotta on toast **18**, 19
  French toast 20, **21**
tomato
  aubergine parmigiana 102, **103**
  baked feta **122**, 123
  baked sweet potatoes **120**, 121

bruschetta 136, **137**
caponata pasta **64**, 65
chicken & chorizo casserole **128**, 129
chicken gyros **116**, 117
chickpea stew 124, **125**
farinata 28, **29**
gigantes plaki **36**, 37
Greek salad 94, **95**
harissa beef meatballs 84, **85**
herby couscous stuffed peppers 62, **63**
lentil ragù **126**, 127
minestrone **130**, 131
pan con tomate 24, **25**
pitta nachos **142**, 143
ratatouille 112, **113**
seafood paella **86**, 87
slow-cooked lamb shoulder **104**, 105
spaghetti vongole **88**, 89
Spanish-style fish stew 54, **55**
spiced butternut squash tagine **72**, 73
spinach fritters **96**, 97
tabbouleh salad 56, **57**
tuna niçoise salad **42**, 43
turkey kebabs 80, **81**
see also passata
tortilla, Spanish **40**, 41
tortilla wraps, halloumi 44, **45**
tuna niçoise salad **42**, 43
turkey kebabs 80, **81**

Turkish eggs **30**, 31
tzatziki 148, **149**

V
vine leaves, dolmades **138**, 139
vongole, spaghetti **88**, 89

W
walnut
  baklava bites **156**, 157
  caponata pasta **64**, 65
  figs with ricotta on toast **18**, 19
  Greek yogurt bark 168, **169**
  honey cake 154, **155**
  pesto 48, **49**, 136, **137**
  watermelon & halloumi salad 38, **39**
watermelon
  watermelon & halloumi salad 38, **39**
  watermelon granita 162, **163**
wraps, halloumi 44, **45**

Y
yogurt
  orange olive oil cake **152**, 153
  roasted potato salad **52**, 53
  see also Greek yogurt

About the authors

Susanna Unsworth is a chef, food stylist, and writer based in London. She trained at Leiths School of Food and Wine.

Laura Clark is a registered dietitian and nutrition consultant. You can find out more about Laura's work at themenopausedietitian.co.uk and on Instagram @menopause.dietitian.

Publisher's acknowledgments

DK would like to thank Laura Clark for nutritional consultancy, Maisie Chandler and Susannah Cohen for assistance with food styling, Kathryn Glendenning for proofreading, and Lisa Footitt for providing the index.

DK LONDON

Editorial Director Cara Armstrong
Project Editor Izzy Holton
Design Manager Tania Gomes
Designer Izzy Poulson
Senior Production Controller Stephanie McConnell
DTP and Design Coordinator Heather Blagden
Art Director Maxine Pedliham
Publishing Director Stephanie Jackson

Author, Recipe Development, and Food Styling Susanna Unsworth
Design Abi Harshorne
Editorial Kate Reeves-Brown
Photography Anthony Duncan
Prop Styling Charlie Phillips

DK DELHI

Art Editor Devina Pagay
Senior Art Editor Ira Sharma
Project Editor Ankita Gupta
Managing Editor Saloni Singh
Managing Art Editor Neha Ahuja Chowdhry
Pre-production designer Satish Chandra Gaur
Pre-production and DTP Coordinator Pushpak Tyagi
Pre-production Manager Balwant Singh
Production Manager Pankaj Sharma
Creative Head Malavika Talukder

First published in Great Britain in 2026 by
Dorling Kindersley Limited
20 Vauxhall Bridge Road,
London SW1V 2SA

The authorised representative in the EEA is
Dorling Kindersley Verlag GmbH. Arnulfstr. 124,
80636 Munich, Germany

Copyright © 2025 Dorling Kindersley Limited A Penguin Random House Company
10 9 8 7 6 5 4 3 2 1
001–356111–April/2026

All rights reserved.
No part of this publication may be reproduced, stored in or introduced into a retrieval system, or transmitted, in any form, or by any means (electronic, mechanical, photocopying, recording, or otherwise), without the prior written permission of the copyright owner. DK values and supports copyright. Thank you for respecting intellectual property laws by not reproducing, scanning or distributing any part of this publication by any means without permission.
By purchasing an authorised edition, you are supporting writers and artists and enabling DK to continue to publish books that inform and inspire readers.
No part of this publication may be used or reproduced in any manner for the purpose of training artificial intelligence technologies or systems. In accordance with Article 4(3) of the DSM Directive 2019/790, DK expressly reserves this work from the text and data mining exception.

A CIP catalogue record for this book is available from the British Library.
ISBN: 978-0-2417-8999-5

Printed and bound in China

www.dk.com